THE LONGMAN INVESTMENT COMPANION

A Comparative Guide to Market Performance

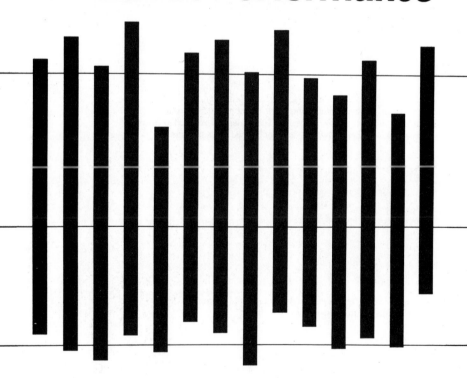

Gordon K. Williamson

Longman Financial Services Publishing
a division of Longman Financial Services Institute, Inc.

This book is dedicated to my parents, Ann Granger Williamson and Murray Deming Williamson, for the patience and wisdom they have taught me. Their continuous support and love have made my life a real joy.

I would like to acknowledge the time, effort and expertise of associate Gregory J. Baker, the chief research assistant for this book.

While a great deal of care has been taken to provide accurate and current information, the ideas, suggestions, general principles and conclusions presented in this book are subject to local, state and federal laws and regulations, court cases and any revisions of same. The reader is thus urged to consult legal counsel regarding any points of law—this publication should not be used as a substitute for competent legal advice.

Executive Editor: Kathleen A. Welton
Project Editor: Lois Smit
Interior Design: Edwin Harris
Cover Design: Vito De Pinto Graphic Design, Inc.

© 1989 by Longman Group USA Inc.

Published by Longman Financial Services Publishing
a division of Longman Financial Services Institute, Inc.

Printed in the United States of America.

89 90 91 10 9 8 7 6 5 4 3 2

Library of Congress Cataloging-in-Publication Data

Williamson, Gordon K.
    The Longman investment companion : a comparative guide to market performance / Gordon K. Williamson.
        p. cm.
    Includes index.
    ISBN 0-88462-832-9
    1. Investments   2. Investment analysis   I. Longman Financial
Services Publishing.   II. Title.
HG4521.W484   1989
332.6—dc19   88-35584
                                            CIP

CONTENTS

INTRODUCTION

The Longman Investment Companion is an essential reference book for anyone who gives or seeks financial advice, including stockbrokers, financial planners, accountants, bankers, real estate brokers, insurance agents and individual investors.

This book was written to fill a void. A tremendous need exists for a reliable, unbiased and comprehensive review of the major investment vehicles. While there are dozens of books on different investments, the vast majority of them are biased toward a specific topic or strategy. The problem with many of these "sources" is that they approach their particular subject in a vacuum or use a select period of time when an investment performed in a very positive manner. Obviously, virtually all investments have performed well during at least some period of time. But, in order to make a wise investment decision, one needs an accurate picture of how the vehicle has performed over a substantial time frame that includes good and bad markets, high and low interest rates, and a wide variety of economies. It is also essential to be able to compare the performances of different investment vehicles within that same time frame and against the same measures.

As an investment counselor, teacher and writer on financial matters, I have experienced a tremendous sense of frustration due to the lack of such an objective resource. I was continually spending a great deal of time and energy in tracking down past performance figures only to discover that agencies and sources that one would think should keep annual figures simply do not, and that I was obliged to consult dozens of different books, periodicals and charts to obtain the information I needed. Thus, I decided to fill the void by writing this book.

The chapters of this book are arranged alphabetically, by investment vehicle, to include bonds, currencies, interest rates, market indicators, mutual funds, stocks and tangibles. Each section contains a description and background information on the investment being studied, followed by a chart that shows how the particular investment has performed, in most cases, over the past twenty-one years.* The accompanying table then breaks down the specific performance figures on a year-by-year basis. Finally, the average annual return at the bottom of each table gives the average performance of the vehicle over the period noted. The latter is intended as a gauge of how the instrument may act in the future over the long term.

Investors concerned with shorter time frames should emphasize the most recent three to five years. Conservative investors may wish to study those years in which the asset did particularly well and, more important, badly. I should add that the chapters on currencies (missing from most investment guides) provide an important measure against which to evaluate one's investment choices, as the value and trading of currencies throughout the world have a direct effect on every investment vehicle presented.

*Almost all of the charts in this book cover each of the past 21 years (1968–1989). The choice of a 21-year time frame was not based on any statistical formula or historical event, but rather the belief that 21 years represented a substantial period of time that included high and low interest rates, good and bad markets, and every possible economy except a depression. For investments and instruments that have been in existence for less than 21 years, the time period including the inceptions of such items was used. A few of the tables and charts do not cover 21 years because such information could not be obtained by the author or his researcher.

Historical performance figures are only one of several criteria that should be used in the investment-selection process. However, as all investors want to know how an investment has performed before making a financial commitment to it, we have provided performance data on more than seventy investments; and, except where noted, all the information contained in this book is from unbiased sources. My chief research assistant and I obtained this information from a wide range of government agencies, mutual fund source books, newsletters, international investment guides, written correspondence and telephone conversations with sources believed to be leaders in their respective fields.

There is no one best investment to choose or strategy to follow. Presumably, if there were such a number-one performer, all of us would place our monies with this ''winner.'' Unfortunately, last year's or the last decade's number-one investment rarely turns out to be on top during the next period. Therefore, investors would be wise to review their own goals, objectives, expected holding periods, tax brackets, current holdings and risk level. A great number of investments can be eliminated once these factors have been considered. It is also extremely important to note that the different parts of a portfolio do not all move up and down together. The charts and tables in this text show such correlations and will aid the investor in balancing a portfolio, on an ongoing basis, for the best possible returns. It is our goal that this book address some of the most important considerations in selecting an investment.

BONDS

Canadian Government Bonds

Canada is a member of the "Group of Seven." Representatives to this group, which also includes Great Britain, France, West Germany, Italy, Japan and the United States, meet several times a year to discuss economic issues.

From 1960 to 1980, Canadian government bonds had a compound average annual return of 3.3 percent in U.S.-dollar terms. A dollar invested in these bonds in 1960 would have been worth $1.99 at the end of this 20-year period.

Standard deviation measures the risk level of an investment. The higher the standard deviation, the greater the risk. As a reference point, one-year bank CDs have a standard deviation of less than three, whereas aggressive-growth funds have a standard deviation of over 20.

The standard deviation for Canadian government bonds for this time frame was 6.3 percent.

The correlation between Canadian bonds and U.S. bonds is quite high at .632. (A perfect correlation in degree and direction of movement would be 1.00.)

The accompanying chart and graph represent returns on Canadian government bonds over the past several years in U.S.-dollar terms. The maturity of this bond portfolio is ten years.

Additional Information

Canadian Business Magazine. CB Media Limited, 70 the Esplanade, 2nd floor, Toronto M5E IR2, Ontario, Canada.

CANADIAN GOVERNMENT BONDS

Year	Annual Total Return	Cumulative Total
1978	-5.5%	-6%
1979	-0.6%	-7%
1980	1.7%	-5%
1981	-2.4%	-7%
1982	35.7%	26%
1983	9.6%	39%
1984	8.8%	52%
1985	17.5%	79%
1986	17.2%	109%
1987	8.6%	228%
1988	20.0%	294%

Average compound annual return for the last 11 years = 13.3%.

United Kingdom Government Bonds

Foreign bonds often take nicknames from their country of issuance; British bonds are called *Bulldog bonds*. The United Kingdom is a member of the Group of Seven. Representatives to this group, which also includes Canada, France, West Germany, Italy, Japan and the United States, meet several times a year to discuss economic issues.

From 1960 to 1980, British government bonds had a compound average annual return of 5.9 percent in U.S.-dollar terms. A dollar invested in these bonds in 1960 would have been worth $3.32 at the end of this 20-year period.

The standard deviation for this time frame was 14.9 percent.

The correlation between British bonds and U.S. bonds is quite low at .076. (A perfect correlation in degree and direction of movement would be 1.00.)

The accompanying chart and graph represent returns on U.K. government bonds over the past several years in U.S.-dollar terms. The maturity of this bond portfolio is ten years. As a point of comparison, stocks in Great Britain had an average dividend yield of 4.1 percent at the beginning of 1989.

Additional Information

The Economist. 54 St. James Street, London SW 1A 1PJ, England.

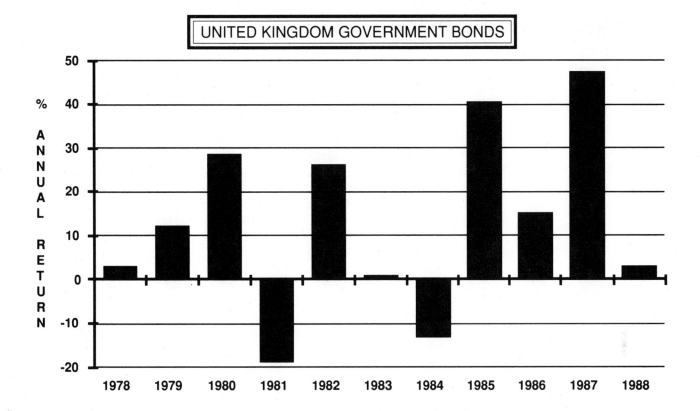

Year	Annual Total Return	Cumulative Total
1978	3.2%	3%
1979	12.4%	15%
1980	28.9%	48%
1981	-19.0%	20%
1982	26.5%	52%
1983	1.0%	54%
1984	-13.1%	34%
1985	40.6%	89%
1986	15.3%	117%
1987	47.5%	221%
1988	3.0%	231%

Average compound annual return for the last 11 years = 11.5%.

French Government Bonds

France is a member of the Group of Seven. Representatives to this group, which also includes the United States, West Germany, Japan, Italy, Great Britain and Canada, meet several times a year to discuss economic issues.

From 1960 to 1980, French government bonds had a compound average annual return of 5.3 percent in U.S.-dollar terms. A dollar invested in these bonds in 1960 would have been worth $2.95 at the end of this 20-year period.

The standard deviation for this time frame was 12.3 percent. (Standard deviation measures the risk level of an investment. The higher the standard deviation, the greater the risk. As a reference point, money market funds have a standard deviation of less than 3, whereas metals funds have a standard deviation of over 40.)

The correlation between French bonds and U.S. bonds is quite low at .146.

The accompanying chart and graph represent returns on French government bonds over the past several years in U.S.-dollar terms. The maturity of this bond portfolio is ten years. As a point of comparison, French stocks had an average dividend yield of 2.2 percent at the beginning of 1989.

Additional Information

International Update. First National Bank of Chicago, Business and Economic Research Division, 1 First National Plaza, Chicago, IL 60670. (312) 732-3779.

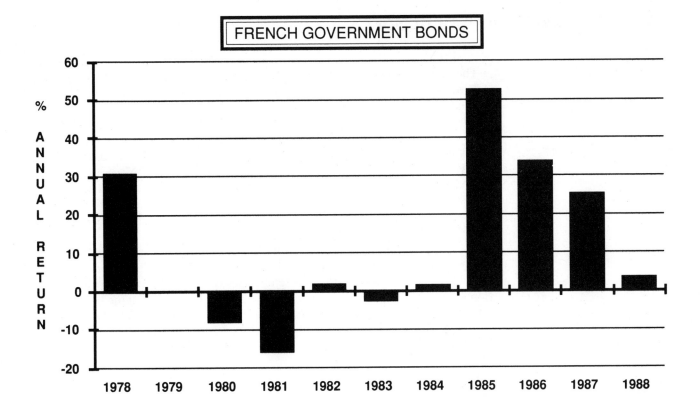

FRENCH GOVERNMENT BONDS

Year	Annual Total Return	Cumulative Total
1978	31.1%	31%
1979	0.2%	31%
1980	-8.1%	21%
1981	-16.1%	2%
1982	1.9%	4%
1983	-2.8%	1%
1984	1.6%	3%
1985	52.7%	58%
1986	33.9%	112%
1987	25.4%	165%
1988	3.7%	176%

**Average compound annual return for the last
11 years = 9.7%.**

West German Government Bonds

The Federal Republic of Germany is a member of the Group of Seven. From 1960 to 1980, West German government bonds had a compound average annual return of 10.3 percent in U.S.-dollar terms. A dollar invested in these bonds in 1960 would have been worth $7.77 at the end of this 20-year period.

The standard deviation for this time frame was 9.2 percent. (Standard deviation measures the risk level of an investment. The higher the standard deviation, the greater the risk. As a reference point, the AMEX has a standard deviation of approximately 27, whereas municipal bonds have a standard deviation of 8.)

The correlation between German bonds and U.S. bonds is quite low at .098.

The accompanying chart and graph represent returns on West German government bonds over the past several years in U.S.-dollar terms. The maturity of this bond portfolio is ten years. As a point of comparison, West German stocks had an average dividend yield of 2.2 percent at the beginning of 1989.

Additional Information

Monthly Reports of the Bundesbank. Deutsche Bundesbank, P.O. Box 10 06 02, D-6000 Frankfurt 1, West Germany.

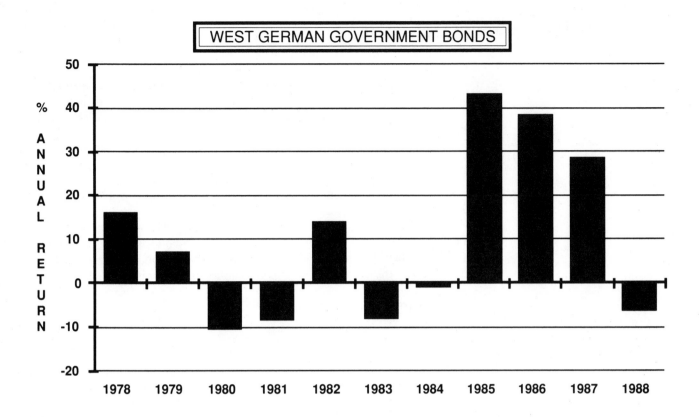

WEST GERMAN GOVERNMENT BONDS

Year	Annual Total Return	Cumulative Total
1978	16.2%	16%
1979	7.4%	24%
1980	-10.6%	10%
1981	-8.4%	1%
1982	14.1%	15%
1983	-8.1%	6%
1984	-1.0%	5%
1985	43.4%	50%
1986	38.7%	109%
1987	28.7%	170%
1988	-6.3%	154%

Average compound annual return for the last 11 years = 8.8%.

Japanese Government Bonds

Foreign bonds often take nicknames from their country of issuance; Japanese bonds are called *Samurai bonds*. Japan is a member of the Group of Seven.

From 1960 to 1980, Japanese government bonds had a compound average annual return of over 10 percent in U.S.-dollar terms. A dollar invested in these bonds in 1960 would have been worth $8.26 at the end of this 20-year period.

The standard deviation for this time frame was 11.9 percent.

The correlation between Japanese bonds and U.S. bonds is quite low at .095.

The accompanying chart and graph represent returns on Japanese government bonds over the past several years in U.S.-dollar terms. The maturity of this bond portfolio is ten years. As a point of comparison, Japanese stocks had an average dividend yield of 0.5 percent at the beginning of 1989.

Additional Information

Japan Economic Journal. Tokyo International, P.O. Box 5004, Tokyo, Japan.

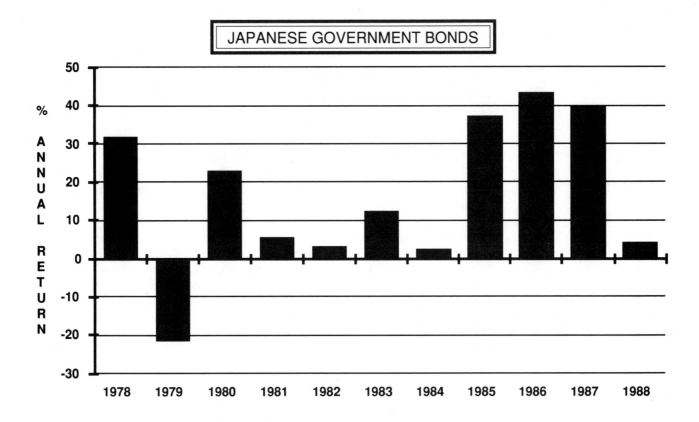

JAPANESE GOVERNMENT BONDS

Year	Annual Total Return	Cumulative Total
1978	31.9%	32%
1979	-21.5%	3%
1980	22.9%	27%
1981	5.5%	35%
1982	3.3%	39%
1983	12.5%	57%
1984	2.7%	62%
1985	37.3%	122%
1986	43.6%	220%
1987	39.9%	348%
1988	4.2%	366%

Average compound annual return for the last 11 years = 15.0%.

Swiss Government Bonds

Unlike Eurobonds, foreign bonds are issued by foreign borrowers and are denominated in that nation's currency. Close to 2.5 percent of all foreign bonds are issued in Switzerland. The value of the outstanding Swiss government bond market is close to $6 billion. Switzerland is not a member of the Group of Seven.

From 1960 to 1980, Swiss government bonds had a compound average annual return of 8.4 percent in U.S.-dollar terms. A dollar invested in these bonds in 1960 would have been worth almost $5.50 at the end of this 20-year period.

The standard deviation for this time frame was 12.4 percent.

The correlation between Swiss bonds and U.S. bonds is extremely low at .059.

The accompanying chart and graph represent returns on Swiss government bonds over the past several years in U.S.-dollar terms. The maturity of this bond portfolio is ten years. As a point of comparison, Swiss stocks had an average dividend yield of 2.2 percent at the beginning of 1989.

Additional Information

Swiss Bank Corporation. 2 Rue de la Confederation, Ch-1204 Geneva, Switzerland.
(022) 37 67 25.

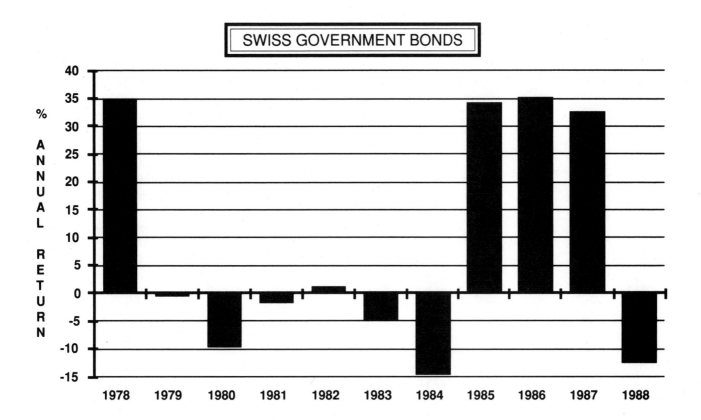

Year	Annual Total Return	Cumulative Total
1978	34.7%	35%
1979	-0.6%	34%
1980	-9.6%	21%
1981	-1.7%	19%
1982	1.2%	20%
1983	-4.8%	14%
1984	-14.7%	-3%
1985	34.4%	30%
1986	35.2%	76%
1987	32.6%	134%
1988	-12.5%	104%

Average compound annual return for the last 11 years = 6.7%.

World Bond Index

From 1960 to 1984, the world bond index had a compound average annual return of just over 6 percent in U.S.-dollar terms. A dollar invested in these bonds in 1960 would have been worth approximately $4.50 at the end of this 25-year period.

The standard deviation over this time frame was 5.56 percent.

The correlation between foreign government bonds and U.S. government bonds is low at .117. The correlation between the world bond index and U.S. bonds is quite high at .646. (A perfect correlation in degree and direction of movement would be 1.00.)

A great deal of misinformation has been written about the burden and impact of the U.S. debt. Any type of debt should be measured in relation to a country's ability to pay back such loans — in other words, its GNP. The U.S. national debt, as a percentage of its GNP, ranks about average in comparison with other members of the Group of Seven. At approximately 55 percent of the GNP, America's national debt ranks above that of Germany (approx. 42 percent), France (approx. 45 percent) and the United Kingdom (approx. 52 percent), but dramatically below that of Japan (approx. 70 percent), Canada (approx. 71 percent) and Italy (approx. 90 percent). The U.S. national debt, also known as gross federal debt, peaked at 127 percent of GNP in 1946. It stood at about 30 percent after World War I, reached a low of 2 percent in 1916 and was 16 percent just before the Depression.

Some critics believe that the true culprit is not the national debt (which in the United States is currently at the same level it was under President Kennedy) but the strain of interest payments on such debt. Measurement should be based on a compilation of a country's federal, state and municipal revenues and debt. Compared to other members of the Group of Seven, the United States is in the middle of the pack. With an overall interest payment burden of 2.2 percent of GNP, the United States ranks behind Japan (1.7 percent) and France (2.1 percent), even with West Germany (2.2 percent), and better off than the United Kingdom (2.7 percent), Canada (3.9 percent) or Italy (7.4 percent).

The accompanying chart and graph represent returns over the past several years in U.S.-dollar terms. The maturity of this bond portfolio is ten years.

Additional Information

Schweizerische Nationalbank Monatsbericht. Orell Fussli Graphische Betriebe, 8036 Zurich 3, Switzerland.

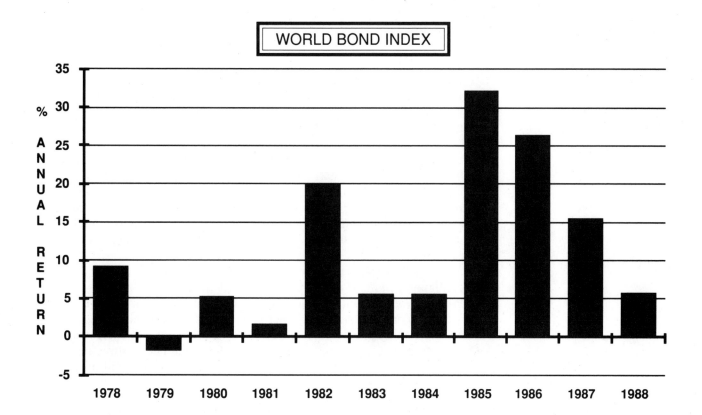

Year	Annual Total Return	Cumulative Total
1978	9.2%	9%
1979	-1.8%	7%
1980	5.4%	12%
1981	1.7%	14%
1982	20.2%	37%
1983	5.7%	45%
1984	5.7%	54%
1985	32.2%	103%
1986	26.5%	158%
1987	15.6%	199%
1988	5.9%	217%

Average compound annual return for the last 11 years = 11.1%.

United States Treasury Bills

United States Treasury bills (T-bills) represent the largest part of the negotiable debt of the U.S. government. They are secured by the federal government's full faith and credit and are issued weekly with original-issue maturities of 13, 26 and 52 weeks. Treasury bills are always issued at a discount from face value. The difference between purchase price and face value is considered interest income. The income from Treasury securities is exempt from state and local, but not federal, taxes.

T-bills are issued in minimum denominations of $10,000, with $5,000 increments thereafter. T-bills, like T-notes and T-bonds, can be purchased through financial institutions or directly from the Treasury. Direct purchases are accomplished by sending a certified check directly to a Federal Reserve Bank.

Treasury bills are the primary vehicle used by the Federal Reserve System in regulating the money supply. This is part of the process referred to as *open-market operations*. By purchasing T-bills for its own account, the Fed is freeing up private capital for other investments and expenditures. Such a move is considered a sign that the Fed is trying to stimulate the economy. On the other hand, by keeping interest rates high, the Fed is attracting purchasers of federal securities. Investors who purchase T-bills will have less funds to purchase goods and services. This type of action is designed to be deflationary.

Economists define the short-term, real-riskless interest rate as the Treasury-bill yield minus anticipated inflation. Over the past half century, the short-term, real-riskless rate of interest has averaged less than one-third of one percent. Over the past three decades, real returns have increased and the real-riskless rate is now considered to be around one percent annually. During the 1980s, the real-riskless rate has risen to record levels.

Additional Information

Department of the Treasury, Bureau of Public Debt Information Center. 13th and C Streets, SW, Washington, DC 20228. (202) 287-4091.

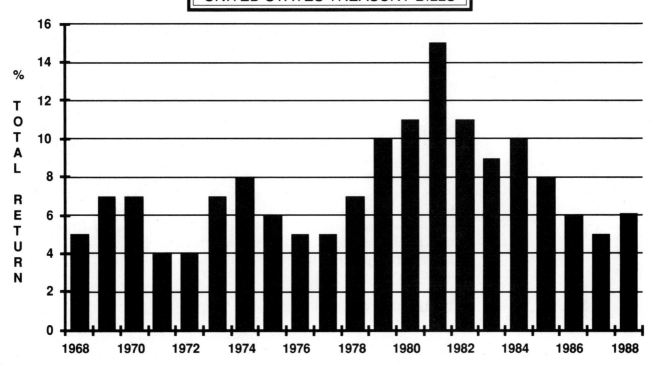

Year	Annual Total Return	Cumulative Total
1968	5%	5%
1969	7%	12%
1970	7%	20%
1971	4%	25%
1972	4%	30%
1973	7%	39%
1974	8%	50%
1975	6%	59%
1976	5%	67%
1977	5%	75%
1978	7%	87%
1979	10%	106%
1980	11%	129%
1981	15%	163%
1982	11%	192%
1983	9%	218%
1984	10%	250%
1985	8%	278%
1986	6%	301%
1987	5%	321%
1988	6%	346%

Average compound annual return for the last 21 years = 7.4%.

Intermediate-Term Government Bonds

Intermediate-term bonds, also known as *medium-term bonds,* are usually defined as debt instruments that have remaining maturities ranging from six to 15 years. Short-term bonds are defined as those with maturities of five years or less. Long-term bonds are those debt instruments with remaining maturities of 16 years or more.

Studies have shown that bonds with relatively modest maturities, ranging from five to seven years, have higher returns than securities with very short maturities with little additional interest-rate risk. More surprisingly, intermediate-term bonds have had a greater *total* return over the last 60 years than long-term bonds and they have only experienced half of the volatility. The *current* yield on long-term bonds is almost always greater than on medium-term securities; however, *total* return takes into account interest payments as well as the value of the underlying security at any given point in time. Intermediate-term government bonds are one of the few investments that have had a positive current yield and total return each year, over the past half century.

Additional Information

Department of the Treasury, Bureau of Public Debt Information Center. 13th and C Streets, SW, Washington, DC 20228. (202) 287-4088.

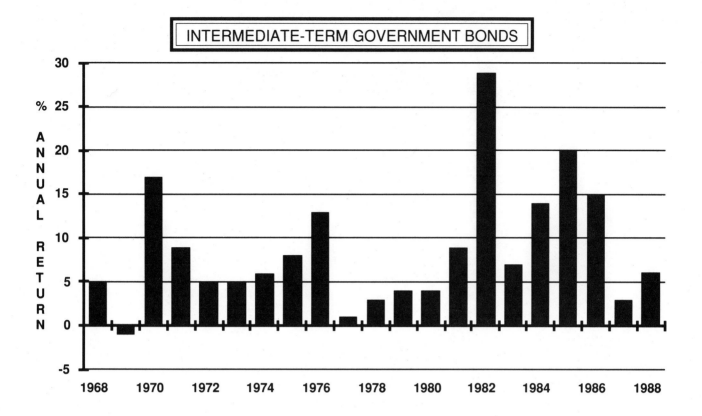

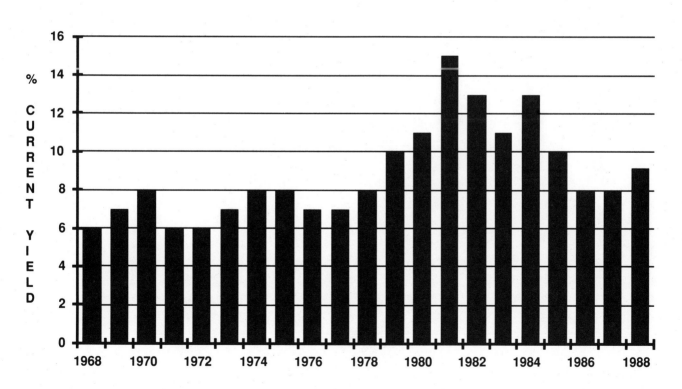

INTERMEDIATE-TERM GOVERNMENT BONDS

Year	Annual Total Return	Current Yield	Cumulative Total
1968	5%	6%	5%
1969	-1%	7%	4%
1970	17%	8%	22%
1971	9%	6%	33%
1972	5%	6%	40%
1973	5%	7%	47%
1974	6%	8%	56%
1975	8%	8%	68%
1976	13%	7%	90%
1977	1%	7%	92%
1978	3%	8%	98%
1979	4%	10%	106%
1980	4%	11%	114%
1981	9%	15%	133%
1982	29%	13%	201%
1983	7%	11%	222%
1984	14%	13%	267%
1985	20%	10%	340%
1986	15%	8%	406%
1987	3%	8%	421%
1988	6%	9%	452%

Average compound annual return for the last 21 years = 8.5%.

Long-Term Government Bonds

Bonds are financial instruments, or securities, from which investors receive interest income on a semiannual basis. The amount of interest paid by the bond issuer is known as the *coupon rate*. Because these contracts have a fixed date of maturity and a predetermined schedule of interest payments, they are known as *fixed-income securities*. Upon maturity, the investor receives back the full face value of the government bond. This value may be more than or less than what was paid for the instrument, depending on whether the bond was purchased at a discount or a premium. Bonds offered at a discount are purchased for less than $1,000 (face value) each; a bond bought for a premium simply means that it was purchased for more than face value.

Securities of the federal government and its agencies represent the largest sector of the U.S. bond market. Like governments around the world, old U.S. debt is maturing, current debt is being refinanced and new debt is sold to obtain more money. There is no default risk with respect to coupon payments or principal repayment because these obligations are fully guaranteed by the full faith and credit of the U.S. government. In addition to safety, direct federal debt issues such as T-bills, T-notes, T-bonds, EE bonds and HH bonds also have tax advantages. While income from federal securities is subject to federal tax, it is exempt from state and local tax.

Treasury bonds are the federal government's longest maturing instruments, with original issue maturities of ten years or greater. Like Treasury notes, Treasury bonds are issued in denominations starting at $1,000, and are highly marketable.

The return on governnment bonds can be measured in three ways: current yield, yield to maturity and total return.

Current yield is arrived at by simply taking the coupon rate of the bond and dividing it by the purchase price. The column titled ''Current Yield'' on the table and chart that follow shows the coupon rate offered by the Treasury each year on new, 20-year government bonds.

Yield to maturity is determined in a fashion similar to current yield, but adds to this formula any prorated discount or premium above or below face value that is paid for the bond. Yield-to-maturity figures are not shown here.

Total return normally measures the annual return on the bond, adding or subtracting the bond's value at the end of the year to its interest payments. Thus, a bond that declined in value by eight percent during the year would have a total return of two percent if the bond had a coupon rate of ten percent. The column titled ''Annual Total Return'' on the following table shows the total return for long-term government bonds each year.

Each of these measurements is important for different types of investors. The current yield figures indicate how an income-oriented investor would have fared each year, assuming the investor made bond purchases each year. The total return figures, on the other hand, are appropriate measures of performance for an investor who was concerned not only with the interest payments received, but also with the value of the underlying security at the end of each year.

Over the last half century, U.S. bonds have beaten inflation slightly, on at least a pretax basis, but have had substantially lower returns than stocks. Following World War II, U.S. Treasuries and long-term U.S. corporate bonds have had negative returns, on an after-tax, after-inflation basis. Bond returns have made a dramatic comeback in the early and mid-1980s.

The value of a dollar invested in 1789 in U.S. government bonds would have grown to over $5000 by the end of 1987. This result assumes cash flows were reinvested at prevailing yields, and it excludes taxes. All of this growth comes from reinvesting income; an investor would have suffered a *loss* of part of his or her dollar if interest payments were spent. Inflation pushed consumer prices 17-fold over the same 199 years. Thus, long-term bond investors would have beat inflation by roughly three percent per year over the period.

The correlation coefficient between long-term government and corporate bonds is almost perfect. On the other hand, the correlation in movement between government bonds and U.S. stocks is very slight. As a point of comparison, U.S. common stocks had an average dividend yield of 3.5 percent at the beginning of 1989.

Additional Information

Department of the Treasury, Bureau of Public Debt Information Center. 13th and C Streets, SW, Washington, DC 20228. (202) 287-4091.

Board of Governors of the Federal Reserve System, Capital Markets Section, Research and Statistics Division. Washington, DC 20551. (202) 452-3631.

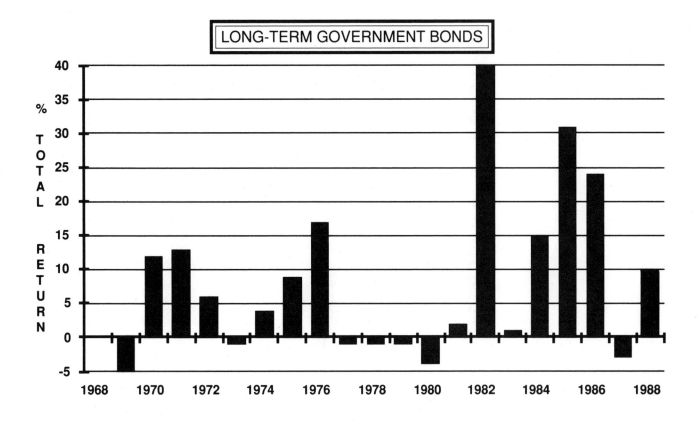

LONG-TERM GOVERNMENT BONDS

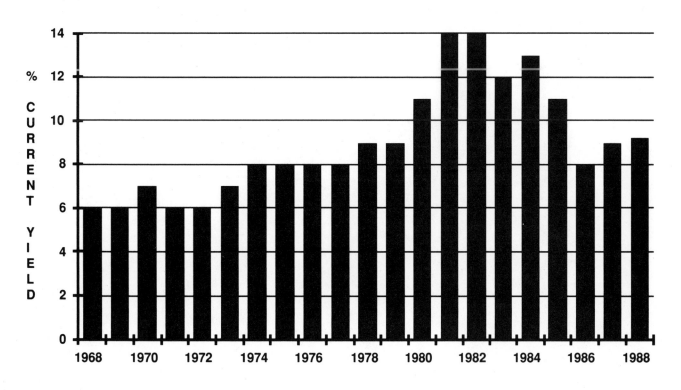

LONG-TERM GOVERNMENT BONDS

Year	Annual Total Return	Current Yield	Cumulative Total
1968	0%	6%	0%
1969	-5%	6%	-5%
1970	12%	7%	6%
1971	13%	6%	20%
1972	6%	6%	27%
1973	-1%	7%	26%
1974	4%	8%	31%
1975	9%	8%	43%
1976	17%	8%	67%
1977	-1%	8%	65%
1978	-1%	9%	63%
1979	-1%	9%	61%
1980	-4%	11%	55%
1981	2%	14%	58%
1982	40%	14%	121%
1983	1%	12%	123%
1984	15%	13%	156%
1985	31%	11%	235%
1986	24%	8%	315%
1987	-3%	9%	303%
1988	10%	9%	343%

Average compound annual return for the last 21 years = 7.3%.

Long-Term Corporate Bonds

Corporate bonds are debt instruments issued by a private entity, as distinguished from bonds issued by a government agency or a municipality. Interest received on these bonds is fully taxable. Corporate bonds are traded on major exchanges and over the counter, with prices published in newspapers.

For the first 150 years of American history, bond yields rose in wartime, corresponding to the inflationary character of such periods. Yields peaked during the War of 1812, the Civil War and World War I. World War II was not associated with an increase in long-term bond yields, even though there were high levels of inflation during the mid-1940s.

After World War II yields started to rise. The yields rose noticeably in the 1950s, increased further in the 1960s and were unprecedentedly high in the 1970s. The practically unbroken rise in yields from 1945 to 1981 represents the most disastrous bond market in North American history. Investors who maintained a constant 20-year-maturity portfolio would have lost two-thirds of their principal due to falling bond prices over that period. This assumes long-term bonds were bought and sold at the end of each year. The dramatic erosion of principal during this period does *not* include the effects of inflation.

Bond losses ended abruptly in 1981. By the middle of 1982, yields were falling even more rapidly than they had risen. Bond prices skyrocketed, but since they were rising from extremely depressed levels, most investors were simply recovering a portion of what they had lost. By the mid-1980s, corporate bond yields, *not total return figures,* had fallen to roughly the same level reached in the late 1970s. The bond market did not turn negative again until 1987.

The value of a country's bonds as a percent of its GNP suggests the degree of leverage of the country's economy. By this measure, the United States, Japan and Switzerland are highly leveraged, with ratios in the 50 percent to 60 percent range. France, on the other hand, has little leverage in its economy: only 17 percent of its GNP. These figures include all outstanding governmental and corporate debt issues.

As a general rule of thumb, when interest rates move an entire point, long-term corporate bonds will change approximately eight percent in value. The value of bonds and interest rates are inversely related; as interest rates move up, the value of a bond goes down, and vice versa. If a bond is held until maturity (and the corporation is still solvent), the full face value of the bond will be repaid. Increases or decreases in the value of bonds is only important if a sale occurs *prior to maturity.*

Over the last half century, the total cumulative return on corporate bonds has been 50 percent greater than government bonds. Both types of bonds have virtually identical standard deviations. The variance of total returns has been less than one-half of that found in a portfolio of S&P 500 stocks.

Additional Information

New York Stock Exchange, Publications Department. 11 Wall Street, New York, NY 10005. (212) 623-2089.

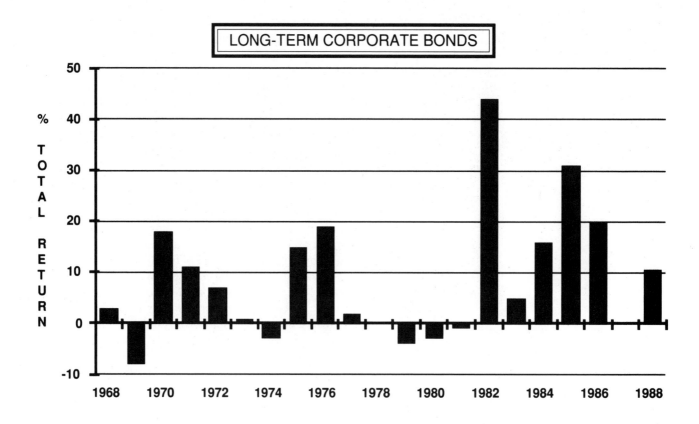

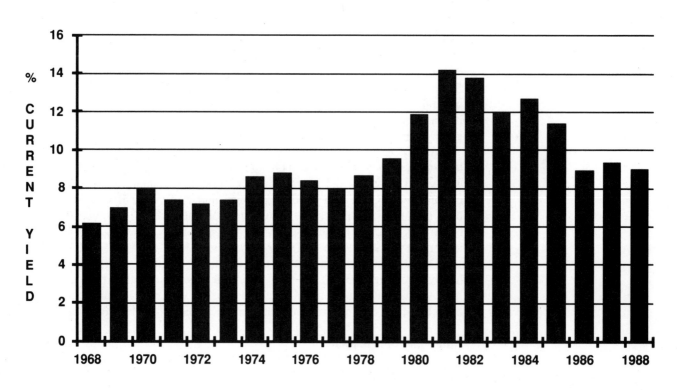

LONG-TERM CORPORATE BONDS

Year	Annual Total Return	Current Yield	Cumulative Total
1968	3%	6.2%	3%
1969	-8%	7.0%	-5%
1970	18%	8.0%	12%
1971	11%	7.4%	24%
1972	7%	7.2%	33%
1973	1%	7.4%	34%
1974	-3%	8.6%	30%
1975	15%	8.8%	50%
1976	19%	8.4%	79%
1977	2%	8.0%	83%
1978	0%	8.7%	83%
1979	-4%	9.6%	76%
1980	-3%	11.9%	71%
1981	-1%	14.2%	69%
1982	44%	13.8%	143%
1983	5%	12.0%	155%
1984	16%	12.7%	196%
1985	31%	11.4%	288%
1986	20%	9.0%	366%
1987	0%	9.4%	366%
1988	11%	9%	417%

Average compound annual return for the last 21 years = 8.1%.

Municipal Bonds (High-Grade AAA)

Municipal bonds are debt obligations of a state or local government entity. The monies raised are used to support general governmental needs or special projects. Issuance must be approved by referendum or by an electoral body. Prior to the Tax Reform Act of 1986, virtually all municipal obligations were exempt from federal income taxes and most were exempt from state and local income taxes, if purchasers bought bonds in their states of residence.

The Tax Reform Act of 1986 categorized some of the municipal issues as *private-purpose bonds*. The interest from private-purpose bonds is taxable unless specifically exempted. Another special category of municipal bonds was created by the 1986 act: *permitted private-purpose bonds*. These bonds are tax-free, but are generally included as tax-preference items when computing the alternative minimum tax (AMT). The AMT is a straight 21 percent; fortunately it only applies to certain wealthy individuals and corporations. All other bonds are classified as *public purpose* and maintain their tax-free status.

Since the overwhelming majority of municipal bonds are classified as public purpose, it is highly unlikely that the individual or corporate investor will come across a municipal bond that is either taxable or included as a tax-preference item. Normally, these "taxable" municipal bonds can be easily spotted since they must pay a higher interest rate in order to attract buyers. Nevertheless, prospective purchasers should always ask their brokers whether the municipal bond in question is something other than a public-purpose issue.

Another means by which municipal bonds are categorized is the way in which interest and principal are to be repaid. There are two major categories within this classification: general obligation (GO) bonds, which are backed by the municipality's full faith and credit, and revenue bonds, which are solely supported by the revenue generated from the project for which the bond was originally issued.

Until the early 1980s, municipal, corporate and government bonds with similar maturities had approximately the same reaction to interest rate changes. Since the mid-1980s, municipal bonds have been only one-half to one-third as volatile as government or corporate bonds, due to the increased demand for municipals and their greatly reduced supply.

Additional Information

Public Securities Association. 40 Broad Street, New York, NY. (212) 809-7000.

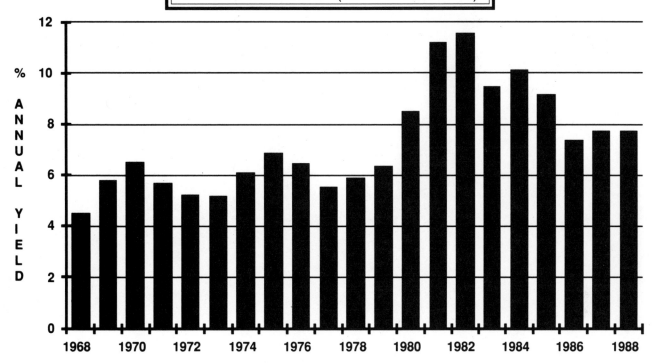

Year	Average Annual Yield	Cumulative Total
1968	4.51%	5%
1969	5.81%	11%
1970	6.51%	18%
1971	5.70%	25%
1972	5.27%	31%
1973	5.18%	38%
1974	6.09%	46%
1975	6.89%	56%
1976	6.49%	65%
1977	5.56%	75%
1978	5.90%	86%
1979	6.39%	97%
1980	8.51%	115%
1981	11.23%	139%
1982	11.57%	168%
1983	9.47%	192%
1984	10.15%	221%
1985	9.18%	250%
1986	7.38%	275%
1987	7.73%	305%
1988	7.75%	337%

Average compound annual yield for the last 21 years = 7.3%.

CURRENCIES

Australian Dollar

Australia's economy has been heavily dependent on its natural resources. This lack of economic diversity is one of the major reasons why this nation's currency and economy have been so volatile. After experiencing a major economic decline that began in the mid-1970s and lasted almost ten years, Australia began to diversify into other industries and experienced a robust rebound in 1985.

More than 100 years ago Australia's per capita income was the highest in the world, 75 percent greater than the United States. The Commonwealth of Australia was formed in the early 1900s. By the end of the 1920s per capita income had fallen below U.S. levels.

Historically, Australia has been known for not promoting free trade. This form of protectionism has hurt its currency as well as its business community. After World War II the country's import and export figures dropped dramatically and stayed low for several decades. After exchange rates were lifted in the early 1970s, the Australian dollar rose close to 30 percent. A few years later, the value of the Australian dollar declined by over 50 percent within a 12-year period. In 1986 the Australian dollar began to strengthen significantly.

Additional Information

ANZ Bank Quarterly Survey. ANZ Bank, 355 Collins Street, Melbourne 3000, Australia.

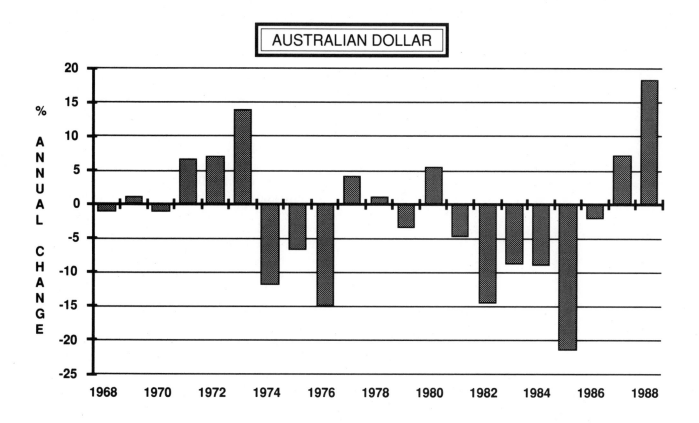

AUSTRALIAN DOLLAR

		Annual	
Year	Aus. $/U.S.$	Change	Cumulative Total
1968	0.90	-1.1%	-1%
1969	0.89	1.1%	0%
1970	0.90	-1.1%	-1%
1971	0.84	6.7%	6%
1972	0.78	7.1%	13%
1973	0.67	14.1%	29%
1974	0.75	-11.9%	14%
1975	0.80	-6.7%	6%
1976	0.92	-15.0%	-10%
1977	0.88	4.3%	-6%
1978	0.87	1.1%	-5%
1979	0.90	-3.4%	-8%
1980	0.85	5.6%	-2%
1981	0.89	-4.7%	-7%
1982	1.02	-14.6%	-21%
1983	1.11	-8.8%	-28%
1984	1.21	-9.0%	-34%
1985	1.47	-21.5%	-49%
1986	1.50	-2.0%	-50%
1987	1.39	7.3%	-46%
1988	1.13	18.4%	-36%

Average compound annual depreciation against the U.S. dollar over the last 21 years = -2.1%.

French Franc

The name of France's currency originated in 1365 with the minting of a coin bearing the likeness of the French king, John II, on horseback. The coin was popularly called *franc à cheval,* "a franc with a horse." At this time the French franc was worth 3.82 grams of gold. By 1423, under Charles VII, the franc had dropped to 3.06 grams of gold.

A century and a half later the French franc was measured in terms of silver, one franc equaling 11.72 grams of fine silver. Close to 30 years later, at the beginning of the seventeenth century, the silver franc was made heavier, but its value had decreased; it now took 23 grams of fine silver to equal one French franc. By 1795 the country's currency had appreciated significantly, a franc equaling only 4.5 fine grams of silver.

The Banque de France was created in 1800 and became the bank that issued the French franc. The bank did not become nationalized until December 2, 1945.

In 1803 a bimetallic monetary system was established in France. A franc could be cashed in for 4.5 fine grams of silver or 290.32 milligrams of fine gold. One U.S. dollar equaled 5.182 French francs. Two years later, limitations on currency convertibility were established, resulting in a maximum depreciation of eight percent.

In 1928 France adopted the gold standard and abolished foreign exchange controls. One U.S. dollar equaled 25.5 French francs. By 1940 it took 43.8 francs to equal one dollar. By the end of 1945, one U.S. dollar bought 119.10 francs. The country's currency continued to depreciate against the dollar until 1960 (350 francs to the dollar in 1949, 420 francs by 1957 and 494 francs to the dollar by 1958).

In 1960 France created the "heavy" or nouveau franc. This restructuring of currency now meant that one U.S. dollar purchased 4.937 nouveau French francs. Three years later, the *nouveau* designation was dropped and the currency was again referred to simply as the *franc.*

In order to maintain fairly level foreign exchange rates, France devalued its currency by 11.1 percent. This devaluation helped somewhat to preserve exchange rates; the dollar was worth 5.554 francs. Near the end of 1969 the French franc hit a low of six francs per U.S. dollar.

Additional Information

International Monetary Fund, Publications Department. 700 19th Street, NW, Washington, DC 20431.

International Market Studies. Foreign Commercial Service, Export Promotion Service, P.O. Box 14207, Washington, DC 20044.

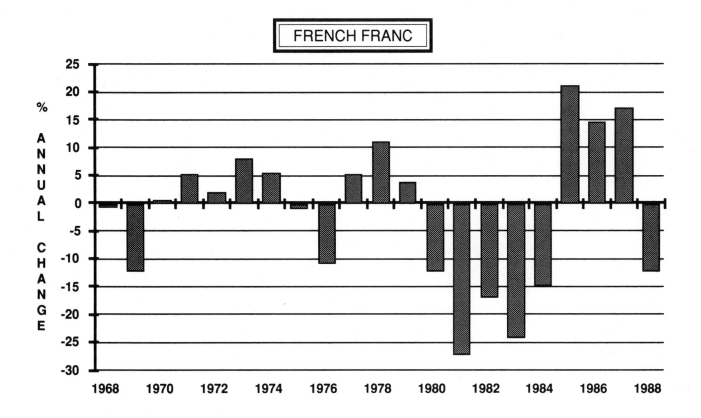

FRENCH FRANC

Year	Francs/$	Annual Change	Cumulative Total
1968	4.9481	-0.8%	-1%
1969	5.5583	-12.3%	-13%
1970	5.5205	0.7%	-12%
1971	5.2245	5.4%	-8%
1972	5.1210	2.0%	-6%
1973	4.7085	8.1%	2%
1974	4.4445	5.6%	8%
1975	4.4855	-0.9%	7%
1976	4.9698	-10.8%	-5%
1977	4.7050	5.3%	0%
1978	4.1800	11.2%	11%
1979	4.0200	3.8%	15%
1980	4.5160	-12.3%	1%
1981	5.7480	-27.3%	-26%
1982	6.7250	-17.0%	-39%
1983	8.3475	-24.1%	-54%
1984	9.5920	-14.9%	-61%
1985	7.5610	21.2%	-53%
1986	6.4550	14.6%	-46%
1987	5.3400	17.3%	-37%
1988	5.9968	-12.3%	-45%

Average compound annual depreciation against the U.S. dollar for the last 21 years = -2.8%. Franc-per-dollar figures represent year-end values.

German Mark

In the twentieth century no currency has suffered a more catastrophic decline than the German mark. At the outbreak of World War I, Germany departed from a gold standard. Between 1914 and 1923 the German mark was devalued by over one-trillionfold. During the period of 1913–1919, the mark dropped over 90 percent in value against the U.S. dollar. Three years later, it took more than 11,000 additional marks to equal that same dollar. This inflation rate is the equivalent of almost six percent daily, compounded each day over the entire year. One year later, it took one trillion marks to receive one dollar bill.

Between 1950 and 1970 the German mark depreciated cumulatively less than one percent over the entire 20-year period. From 1968 to 1988 the German mark reversed direction and shot up in value, almost 90 percent against the U.S. dollar. Overall, since World War II, the German currency has been quite stable in relationship to other currencies.

The following list of monthly reports may be useful to the German-currency trader:

RESERVES: Reported during the middle or end of each week
BALANCE OF TRADE: Issued the first part of the first week of the month
RETAIL SALES: Issued the first part of the first week
COST OF LIVING INDEX: Issued the middle of the third week
UNEMPLOYMENT: Issued the sixth calendar day of the month
WHOLESALE PRICE INDEX: Issued the fourth Tuesday of the month
INDUSTRIAL PRODUCTION INDEX: Issued the latter part of the third week

Additional Information

Loosigian, Allen M. *Foreign Exchange Futures: A Guide To* . . . Homewood, IL: Dow Jones–Irwin, 1981.

Riehl, Heinz and Rita M. Rodriguez. *Foreign Exchange and Money Markets* . . . McGraw-Hill, 1983.

International Financial Statistics. International Monetary Fund, Washington, DC 20431.

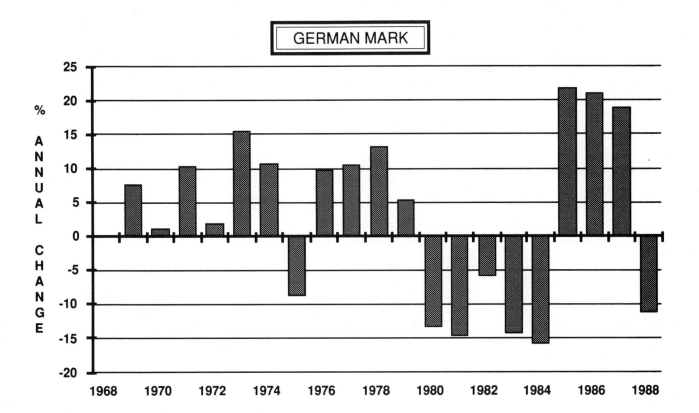

GERMAN MARK

Year	Marks/$	Annual Change	Cumulative Total
1968	4.00	0.0%	0%
1969	3.69	7.8%	8%
1970	3.65	1.1%	9%
1971	3.27	10.4%	20%
1972	3.20	2.1%	22%
1973	2.70	15.6%	42%
1974	2.41	10.7%	58%
1975	2.62	-8.7%	44%
1976	2.36	9.9%	58%
1977	2.11	10.6%	75%
1978	1.83	13.3%	98%
1979	1.73	5.5%	110%
1980	1.96	-13.3%	83%
1981	2.25	-14.8%	56%
1982	2.38	-5.8%	47%
1983	2.72	-14.3%	26%
1984	3.15	-15.8%	6%
1985	2.46	21.9%	29%
1986	1.94	21.1%	56%
1987	1.57	19.1%	86%
1988	1.75	-11.6%	64%

Average compound annual appreciation against the U.S. dollar for the last 21 years = 2.4%. Mark-per-dollar figures represent year-end values.

Italian Lira

The monetary unit of Italy was first issued by the state and five local banks. Due to a bank merger in 1893, only three of the original banks continued to mint the coins. By the middle of 1926 only the Banca d' Italia (Bank of Italy) was allowed to issue the country's currency. The Bank of Italy became nationalized in 1936.

The lira was adopted as the monetary unit of Italy by the House of Savoy in 1862. At this time, one lira equaled 4.5 fine grams of fine silver, or one French franc. Just four years later, the lira began to depreciate from five percent to 20 percent. In 1887 a new series of depreciation began; this time the country's currency lost nine percent of its value. The lira remained relatively stable until 1915.

In 1915 massive loans to the government from the Bank of Italy caused the lira to depreciate 42 percent in 1918, finalizing in a net loss of value of 82 percent in 1920. In 1926 a royal decree was issued, calling for the repayment of loans. A year later the lira was stabilized by devaluing the currency by 72.47 percent. One U.S. dollar equaled 19 lire (plural of lira) in 1927.

In 1936 the government created the tourist lira. This turned out to be the beginning of a series of specialized currencies. These additional currencies, later referred to as *accounts*, lasted until 1959. The lira also depreciated 31 percent in 1936. The lira was again depreciated just a few months later by 41 percent. However, this time the depreciation was in line with that of the U.S. dollar. One dollar still equaled 19 lire. The U.S. dollar parity was lowered to 19.80 lire in 1939. A year later, the creation of a special account lira for regulating transport fees caused the official lira to depreciate 56 percent. United States dollar parity of 19 to one was restored in 1941.

The invasion of Italy by Allied forces resulted in a new official exchange rate of 100 lire to the dollar; by 1946 it took 120 lire to buy one dollar. By the end of 1946, with the authorization of a fluctuating free market, one dollar was worth 509 lire. Less than one year later the black-market rate of lire hit a record 800 per U.S. dollar.

In the middle of 1947 a new official exchange rate was established: one dollar for 350 lire. Two years later the exchange rate had jumped to 625 lire. Due to a series of regulatory actions, this exchange rate was the same in 1960 as it was in 1949. Currency activity remained stable until 1969. From 1969 to 1971, renewed capital flight caused the lira to weaken, hitting a low of 661 per U.S. dollar in 1970. By the end of 1970, conditions improved and the lira began to stabilize at close to 630 per U.S. dollar.

Additional Information

Kubarych, Roger F. *Foreign Exchange Markets in the U.S.* Federal Reserve Bank of New York, 1978.

Walker, Townsend. *A Guide for Using the Foreign Exchange Market*. Wiley, 1981.

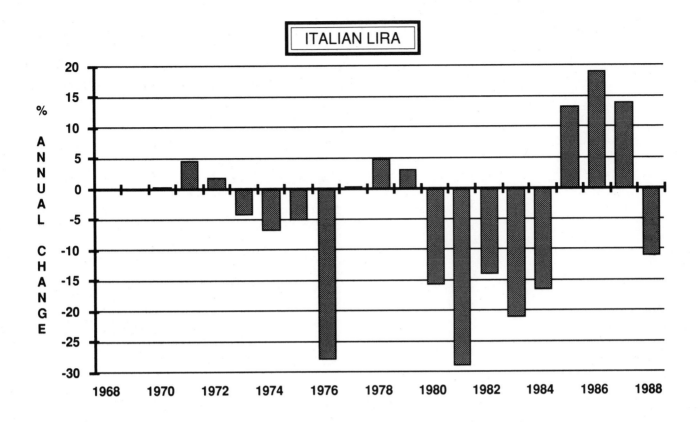

ITALIAN LIRA

Year	Lira/$	Annual Change	Cumulative Total
1968	623.5	0.1%	0%
1969	625.5	-0.3%	0%
1970	623.0	0.4%	0%
1971	594.0	4.7%	5%
1972	582.5	1.9%	7%
1973	607.9	-4.4%	3%
1974	649.4	-6.8%	-4%
1975	683.6	-5.3%	-9%
1976	875.0	-28.0%	-34%
1977	871.6	0.4%	-34%
1978	829.8	4.8%	-31%
1979	804.0	3.1%	-29%
1980	930.5	-15.7%	-40%
1981	1200.0	-29.0%	-57%
1982	1370.0	-14.2%	-63%
1983	1659.5	-21.1%	-71%
1984	1935.9	-16.7%	-76%
1985	1678.5	13.3%	-73%
1986	1358.1	19.1%	-68%
1987	1169.3	13.9%	-64%
1988	1300.3	-11.2%	-68%

Average compound annual depreciation against the U.S. dollar for the last 21 years = -5.3%. Lira-per-dollar figures represent year-end values.

Japanese Yen

The currency of Japan, the yen, has shown a high degree of resiliency since World War II. But the currency's evolution has been impaired by wars and general confusion.

Japan's early currency history was chaotic. The first currencies in Japan were introduced in the mid-1600s. By 1870 more than *1,500* different forms of paper currency were printed in Japan. Nine years later the yen was recognized as the basic unit of currency. After that it took approximately two decades to develop a modern monetary system, first based on silver and then on gold. By 1914 Japan had a gold standard. For over three decades after World War I, Japan's yen floated—unlike much of the rest of the world's currency.

World War II brought Japan to the brink of economic disaster. But recovery was fast and Japan managed to become a world power in trade, enhancing its currency in the process. After World War II Japan switched to a dollar exchange standard that was maintained until 1971, when Japan began to float its yen—a move made in concert with many other world currencies.

During recent years the yen has been the strongest currency in the world. The yen almost doubled in value against the U.S. dollar from 1985 to 1988. Previously the yen was quite stable, trading in the 355-to-360 range for the 20 years ending in 1970. More recently it has proven to be an extremely strong currency.

The following list of monthly reports may be useful to the Japanese-yen trader:

RESERVES: Issued the last day of the month
BALANCE OF TRADE: Issued usually on or close to the 15th
CONSUMER PRICE INDEX: Issued the first part of the first week
WHOLESALE PRICE INDEX: Issued close to the 20th
INDUSTRIAL PRODUCTION INDEX: Issued the first part of the last week
MONEY SUPPLY: Issued the first week

Additional Information

Foreign Exchange and Gold Operations, Department of the Treasury. 15th Street and Pennsylvania Avenue, NW, Room 5037, Washington, DC 20220. (202) 566-2773.

Ensor, Richard and Boris Antl. *Management of Foreign Exchange Risk*. Euromoney Publications, 1983.

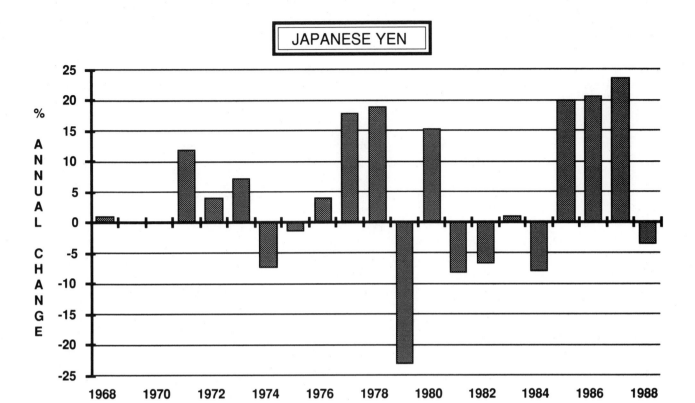

Year	Yen/$	Annual Change	Cumulative Total
1968	357.70	1.2%	1%
1969	357.80	0.0%	1%
1970	357.65	0.0%	1%
1971	314.80	12.0%	13%
1972	302.00	4.1%	18%
1973	280.00	7.3%	26%
1974	300.95	-7.5%	17%
1975	305.15	-1.4%	16%
1976	292.80	4.0%	21%
1977	240.00	18.0%	43%
1978	194.60	18.9%	70%
1979	239.70	-23.2%	31%
1980	203.00	15.3%	51%
1981	219.90	-8.3%	39%
1982	235.00	-6.9%	29%
1983	232.20	1.2%	30%
1984	251.10	-8.1%	20%
1985	200.50	20.2%	44%
1986	159.10	20.6%	74%
1987	121.50	23.6%	116%
1988	125.75	-3.5%	107%

Average compound annual appreciation against the U.S. dollar for the last 21 years = 3.5%. Yen-per-dollar figures represent year-end values.

Swiss Franc

The Swiss franc is well known for its stability and is considered to be a good currency to have in times of extreme crisis. Only once in this century has the Swiss franc been devalued (1934–1936). The sturdiness of the Swiss currency is due largely to Switzerland's lengthy history of continuous neutrality and the fact that until relatively recently over 90 percent of the country's bank notes were backed by gold. That is the highest gold coverage of any currency in the world.

Despite such a historically stellar performance, the Swiss franc has fared poorly recently. From 1980 through 1984 — five consecutive years — the Swiss franc dropped a total of 36 percent against the U.S. dollar. Yet it staged major reversals in 1985, 1986 and 1987. During the past 25 years the Swiss franc has appreciated over the dollar more than twofold. It has appreciated against the U.S. dollar 13 out of the last 20 years.

The following list of monthly reports may be useful to the Swiss franc currency trader:

RESERVES: Weekly reports are issued toward the end of the week
BALANCE OF TRADE: Issued usually on or close to the 17th
CONSUMER PRICE INDEX: Issued usually the eighth or ninth
WHOLESALE PRICE INDEX: Issued the second Friday of the month
MONEY SUPPLY: Issued the first week of the month

Additional Information

International Monetary Fund Publications. 700 19th Street, NW, Washington, DC 20431. (202) 477-7000.

George, Abraham H. and Ian H. Giddy. *International Finance Handbook,* 2 vols. Wiley, 1983.

Solomon, Robert. *The International Monetary System 1945–1976.* Harper and Row, 1977.

Dushek, Charles and Carol Harding. *Trading in Foreign Currencies: Speculative . . .* American TransEuro, 1978.

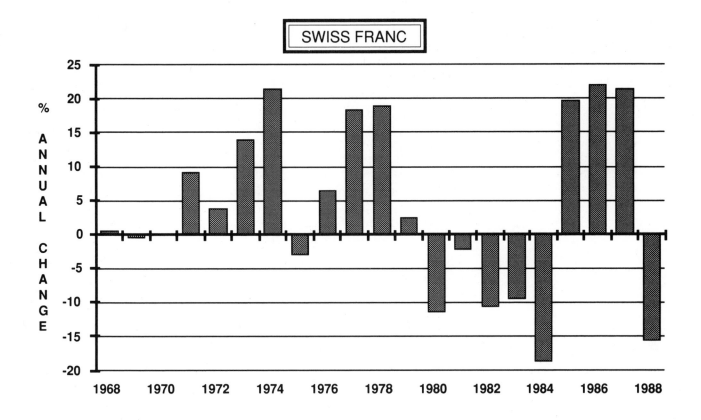

Year	Francs/$	Annual Change	Cumulative Total
1968	4.30	0.7%	1%
1969	4.32	-0.5%	0%
1970	4.32	0.1%	0%
1971	3.92	9.3%	9%
1972	3.77	3.8%	13%
1973	3.24	14.1%	29%
1974	2.54	21.6%	57%
1975	2.62	-3.1%	52%
1976	2.45	6.5%	63%
1977	2.00	18.4%	92%
1978	1.62	19.0%	128%
1979	1.58	2.5%	135%
1980	1.76	-11.4%	109%
1981	1.80	-2.3%	105%
1982	1.99	-10.6%	82%
1983	2.18	-9.5%	64%
1984	2.59	-18.8%	33%
1985	2.08	19.7%	60%
1986	1.62	22.1%	95%
1987	1.27	21.6%	138%
1988	1.47	-15.6%	100%

Average compound annual appreciation against the U.S. dollar for the last 21 years = 3.4%. Franc-per-dollar figures represent year-end values.

United Kingdom Pound

For hundreds of years the British pound sterling was the world's premier currency. Great Britain's posture as an international trader and lender helped make the U.K. pound the most popular currency to own. Except for the U.S. dollar after World War II, no other currency has obtained the stature of the pound in international trade.

Ever since world currencies were allowed to freely float, a move that occurred in the early 1970s, the British pound has been a weak performer. In 1971 the pound was worth more than $2.50 (U.S. dollars), but by 1984 it was as low as $1.10.

The following list of monthly reports may be useful to the British-pound trader:

RESERVES: Issued the first Monday or Tuesday of the month

BALANCE OF TRADE: Issued usually Monday or Tuesday of the fourth week

RETAIL SALES: Issued the first or second Monday

CONSUMER PRICE INDEX: A quarterly report, available at any time

PERSONAL INCOME: Issued the third Wednesday

UNEMPLOYMENT: Issued on Thursday of the fourth week

INDUSTRIAL PRODUCTION INDEX: Issued the third Friday

MONEY SUPPLY: Issued the third week

Additional Information

Foreign Exchange Division, Riggs National Bank. 800 17th Street, NW, Washington, DC 20006. (202) 835-5125.

Coninx, Raymond G.F. *Currency Risk*. Euromoney Publications, 1983.

Einzig, Paul. *A Textbook on Foreign Exchange*. Macmillan, 1969.

Walmsley, J. *The Foreign Exchange Handbook: A User's Guide*. Wiley, 1983.

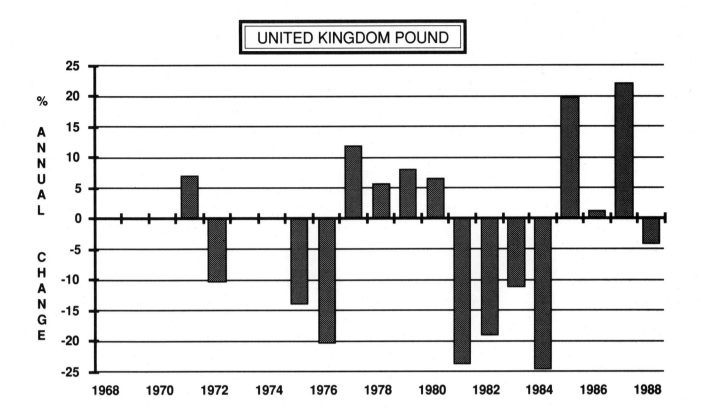

Year	Pound/$	Annual Change	Cumulative Total
1968	0.42	0.0%	0%
1969	0.42	0.0%	0%
1970	0.42	0.0%	0%
1971	0.39	7.1%	7%
1972	0.43	-10.3%	-4%
1973	0.43	0.0%	-4%
1974	0.43	0.0%	-4%
1975	0.49	-14.0%	-17%
1976	0.59	-20.4%	-34%
1977	0.52	11.9%	-26%
1978	0.49	5.8%	-22%
1979	0.45	8.2%	-16%
1980	0.42	6.7%	-10%
1981	0.52	-23.8%	-32%
1982	0.62	-19.2%	-45%
1983	0.69	-11.3%	-51%
1984	0.86	-24.6%	-63%
1985	0.69	19.8%	-56%
1986	0.68	1.4%	-56%
1987	0.53	22.1%	-46%
1988	0.55	-4.2%	-48%

Average compound annual depreciation against the U.S. dollar for the last 21 years = -3.1%. Pound-per-dollar figures represent year end values.

United States Dollar

Until the early 1900s, U.S. currency was issued by privately held banks. The notes held first lien on the issuing bank's assets. In 1907 there was a banking panic. In response to this crisis, the Aldrich-Vreeland Act was passed by Congress in 1908, authorizing a group of specially organized banks to issue emergency bank notes. The Federal Reserve System was created in 1914.

By the early 1930s the United States had abandoned the gold standard; in 1935 bank notes were eliminated. Silver-backed notes were gone by 1963. Today, Federal Reserve notes are obligations of the U.S. government. Since the early 1800s, the U.S. dollar has depreciated 89 percent measured against the price of goods and services.

The amount and volume of currencies traded each day, including the U.S. dollar, is staggering. According to estimates by Morgan Stanley Bank, average daily volume was $425 billion last year. By contrast, on the New York Stock Exchange's biggest day, October 19, 1987, 21 billion dollars' worth of securities changed hands.

The following list of monthly reports may be useful to the U.S.-currency trader:

RESERVES: Reported weekly in New York, usually on late Thursday or Friday afternoon

BALANCE OF TRADE: Issued usually on or close to the 27th

RETAIL SALES: Issued the first part of the second or third week

CONSUMER PRICE INDEX: Issued usually on the 22nd

PERSONAL INCOME: Issued the third Tuesday or Wednesday of the month

LEADING INDICATORS: Issued on the 27th

UNEMPLOYMENT: Issued the first Friday of the month

WHOLESALE PRICE INDEX: Issued in the latter part of the second week

INDUSTRIAL PRODUCTION INDEX: Issued on the 15th

FACTORY AND DURABLE GOODS ORDERS: Issued several times each month at different times

MONEY SUPPLY: Issued weekly on Thursday

Additional Information

Deak Perera. 1800 K Street, NW, Washington, DC 20006. (800) 368-5683.

Aliber, Robert Z. *The International Money Game*. Basic Books, 1979.

Coninx, Raymond G.F. *Foreign Exchange Dealer's Handbook*. Pick Publishing, 1982.

Dufey, Gunter and Ian H. Giddy. *The International Money Market*. Prentice-Hall, 1978.

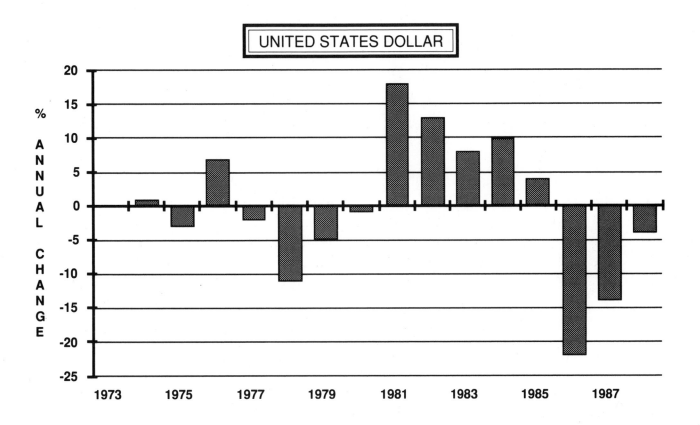

UNITED STATES DOLLAR

Year	Index	Annual Change	Cumulative Total
1973	100.00	0%	0%
1974	101.42	1%	1%
1975	98.50	-3%	-2%
1976	105.63	7%	5%
1977	103.35	-2%	3%
1978	92.39	-11%	-8%
1979	88.07	-5%	-13%
1980	87.39	-1%	-14%
1981	103.26	18%	1%
1982	116.50	13%	14%
1983	125.33	8%	23%
1984	138.34	10%	35%
1985	143.23	4%	40%
1986	112.27	-22%	9%
1987	96.87	-14%	-6%
1988	92.76	-4%	-10%

Average compound annual depreciation for the last 16 years = -0.7%.

Base of 1 is comprised as follows:

6.4%	Belgium	9.1%	Canada
13.1%	France	20.8%	West Germany
9.0%	Italy	13.6%	Japan
8.3%	Netherlands	4.2%	Sweden
3.6%	Switzerland	11.9%	United Kingdom

INTEREST RATES

Certificates of Deposit (CDs)

A CD is an interest-bearing debt instrument issued by a bank or savings and loan association. Institutional CDs, sometimes referred to as *jumbo CDs,* are issued in denominations of $100,000 or more; individual CDs can start as low as $100. Maturities range from a few weeks to several years.

Interest rates offered by these financial institutions are set by competitive forces in the marketplace. When shopping for CDs, prospective investors should be concerned with convenience as well as yield. Interest earned on CDs is fully taxable; form 1099s are sent out at the end of each calendar year.

Most investors are advised to purchase these instruments only from institutions that insure their CDs through the FDIC or FSLIC, agencies created by Congress. Accounts backed by such agencies are insured for losses up to $100,000 per account. Investors who question the solvency of the financial institution should purchase these instruments only in amounts less than $100,000. If the bank or savings and loan association goes bankrupt, investors will want to make sure their principal as well as their interest are protected.

Additional Information

American Bankers Association. 1120 Connecticut Avenue, NW, Washington, DC 20036. (202) 467-4101.

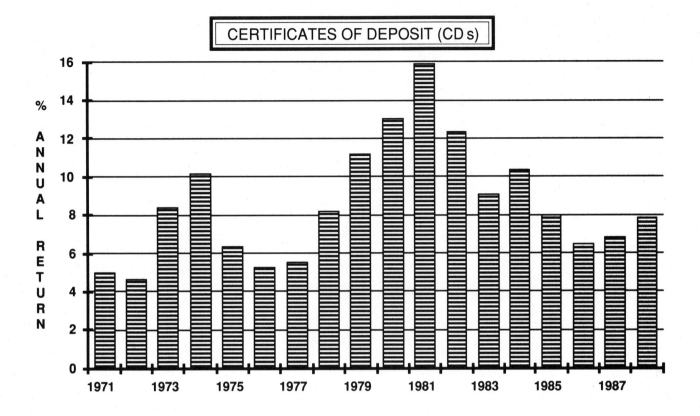

Year	Average Annual Return	Cumulative Total
1971	5.00%	5%
1972	4.70%	10%
1973	8.40%	19%
1974	10.20%	31%
1975	6.40%	39%
1976	5.26%	46%
1977	5.58%	55%
1978	8.20%	67%
1979	11.22%	85%
1980	13.07%	109%
1981	15.91%	142%
1982	12.35%	171%
1983	9.09%	195%
1984	10.37%	225%
1985	8.05%	251%
1986	6.52%	276%
1987	6.87%	302%
1988	7.91%	334%

Average compound annual return for the last 18 years = 8.5%.

Conventional First Mortgages on New Homes

A mortgage is a loan agreement whereby the borrower gives the lender, usually a bank or savings and loan association, a lien on property as security for repayment. Usually mortgages are obtained because the borrower does not have enough money to purchase the property outright. Sometimes mortgages are obtained as a form of leverage or to free up funds for alternative investments. Freeing up cash in order to increase a securities portfolio is recommended for moderate-to-aggressive investors only.

In some states, such as California, residential mortgages are nonrecourse, meaning the lender cannot go after the personal assets of the borrower if the loan is not fully paid back in a timely manner. In essence the lender can only look toward the mortgaged property to satisfy the obligation.

The accompanying graph and table represent the average annual interest rate a borrower would have paid for a home loan during a given year. The interest rates shown do not reflect any up-front points or fees charged by the lender.

Additional Information

Federal Home Loan Bank Board, Office of Communications. 1700 G Street, NW, Washington, DC 20552. (202) 377-6677.

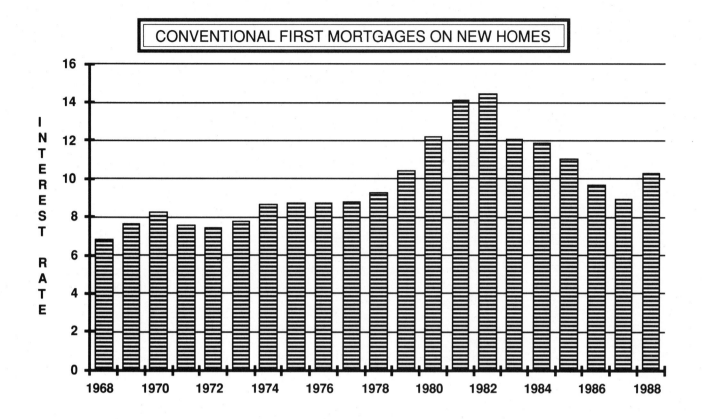

Year	Average Annual Interest Rate
1968	6.8%
1969	7.7%
1970	8.3%
1971	7.6%
1972	7.5%
1973	7.8%
1974	8.7%
1975	8.8%
1976	8.8%
1977	8.8%
1978	9.3%
1979	10.5%
1980	12.3%
1981	14.1%
1982	14.5%
1983	12.1%
1984	11.9%
1985	11.1%
1986	9.7%
1987	8.9%
1988	10.3%*

Average rate for the last 21 years = 9.8%.

* preliminary

Discount Rate

The discount rate is the interest rate that the Federal Reserve charges member banks for loans, using government securities or eligible paper as collateral. This establishes a floor on interest rates, since banks set their loan rates above the discount rate.

The Federal Reserve Board (FRB) is the governing board of the Federal Reserve System. Its seven members are appointed by the president of the United States, subject to Senate confirmation, and serve 14-year terms. The board establishes Federal Reserve policies on key matters such as reserve requirements and other bank regulations. It also sets the discount rate, tightens or loosens the availability of credit in the economy and regulates the purchase of securities on margin.

The *discount window* is a place in the Federal Reserve where banks go to borrow money at the discount rate. Borrowing from the Fed is a privilege, not a right, and banks are discouraged from using the privilege except when they are short of reserves.

Additional Information

The Federal Reserve System, Division of Research and Statistics. Washington, DC 20551. (202) 452-2851.

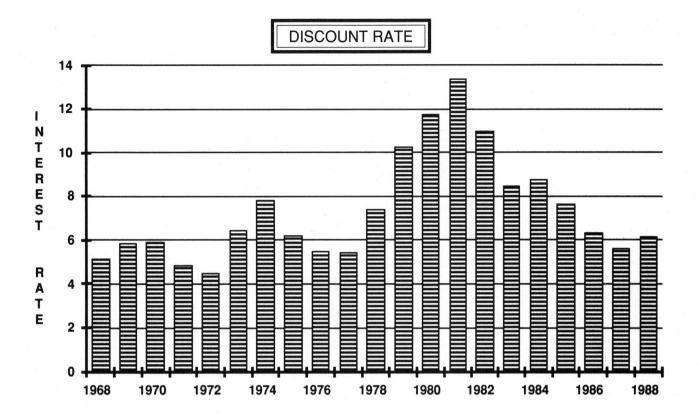

DISCOUNT RATE

Year	Average Annual Interest Rate
1968	5.17%
1969	5.87%
1970	5.95%
1971	4.88%
1972	4.50%
1973	6.45%
1974	7.83%
1975	6.25%
1976	5.50%
1977	5.46%
1978	7.46%
1979	10.28%
1980	11.77%
1981	13.41%
1982	11.02%
1983	8.50%
1984	8.80%
1985	7.69%
1986	6.33%
1987	5.66%
1988	6.20%

Average rate for the last 21 years = 7.38%.

Federal Funds Rate

The phrase *federal funds rate* is somewhat misleading because it sounds as if it is some rate of interest charged by the Federal Reserve System. This is not the case. The federal funds rate is the interest banks with excess reserves charge other banks needing overnight loans to meet reserve requirements. The loans are very short-term in nature.

The federal funds is the most sensitive indicator of the direction of interest rates. The federal funds rate can change during any given day; it is set daily by the market. This is in sharp contrast to the prime and discount rates, which are periodically modified by banks and by the Federal Reserve, respectively.

Additional Information

Bureau of Economic Analysis, U.S. Department of Commerce. Washington, DC 20230.
(202) 523-0777.

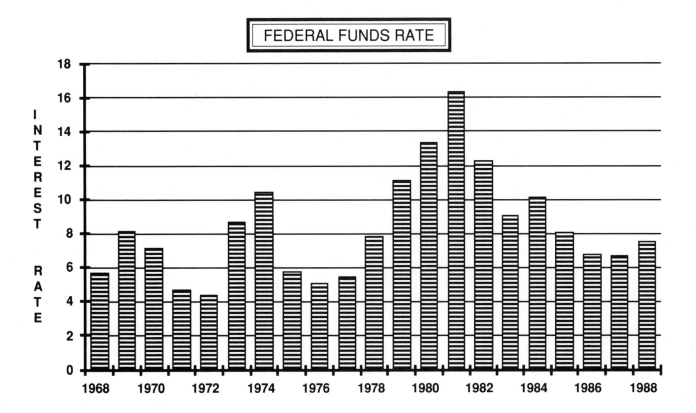

Year	Average Annual Interest Rate
1968	5.7%
1969	8.2%
1970	7.2%
1971	4.7%
1972	4.4%
1973	8.7%
1974	10.5%
1975	5.8%
1976	5.1%
1977	5.5%
1978	7.9%
1979	11.2%
1980	13.4%
1981	16.4%
1982	12.3%
1983	9.1%
1984	10.2%
1985	8.1%
1986	6.8%
1987	6.7%
1988	7.6%

Average rate for the last 21 years = 8.4%.

Prime Rate

The prime rate is the interest rate banks charge their most creditworthy customers. It is also referred to as a bank's *reference rate*. The rate is determined by the market forces affecting a bank's cost of funds, as well as the interest rate acceptable to borrowers. The prime rate tends to become standard across the banking community after a major bank changes its rate.

Although the prime is the rate a financial institution charges its best customers, lenders will sometimes charge businesses a rate of interest that is lower than prime. These below-market levels occur when a bank has excess reserves or is in competition with another lender.

The prime rate has had a varied history. For more than a dozen years the rate stayed at 1.5 percent. By the middle of 1968 it passed six percent for the first time. Its all-time high was 21.5 percent, a level seen briefly in 1980. During one five-year period, 1978–1983, the prime changed over 100 times. The rate has averaged approximately eight percent over the past 25 years.

Additional Information

Money Market Services. 490 El Camino Real, Belmont, CA 94002. (800) 227-7304.

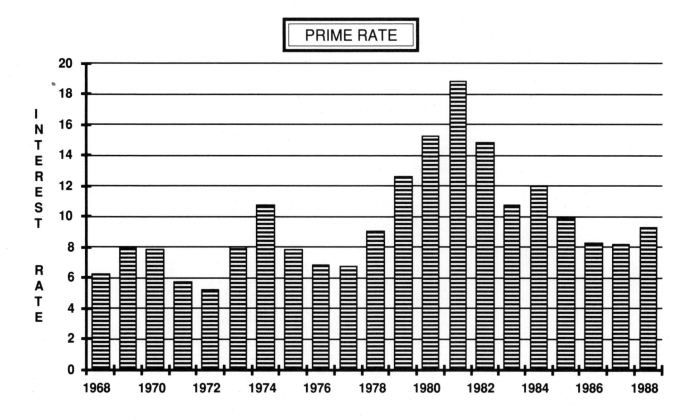

Year	Average Annual Interest Rate	Cumulative Total
1968	6.3%	6%
1969	8.0%	14%
1970	7.9%	23%
1971	5.7%	30%
1972	5.3%	37%
1973	8.0%	48%
1974	10.8%	64%
1975	7.9%	77%
1976	6.8%	89%
1977	6.8%	102%
1978	9.1%	120%
1979	12.7%	149%
1980	15.3%	186%
1981	18.9%	240%
1982	14.9%	291%
1983	10.8%	334%
1984	12.0%	386%
1985	9.9%	435%
1986	8.3%	478%
1987	8.2%	524%
1988	9.3%	580%

Average rate for the last 21 years = 9.6% .

MARKET INDICATORS

Average Price of New One-Family House

Over the past 20 years, enthusiasm for home ownership has greatly intensified. This increased interest has largely been caused by inflation, which has sent the price of the average American home from $25,000 in the early 1960s to over $100,000 by the late 1980s. People who originally purchased homes simply because they needed places to live suddenly found themselves owning investments.

Historically, homes were not considered a way to increase one's wealth. Twenty-five years ago homeowners commonly expected their homes to lose value each year due to wear and tear. Today most people feel that their home has been their best investment.

At least one study shows how home prices nationwide have been slipping in real terms. In this context, *real terms* means the sales price minus adjustments for inflation and home improvements. Using a base of $66,000 in 1970, home prices peaked in 1983, when they reached close to $86,000. Estimates for 1988 place this value down to $79,000. All of these figures are in 1982 dollars.

The rise in home prices nationwide far outstripped inflation in the 1970s, but has actually lagged behind the consumer price index (CPI) when quality improvements (remodeling, air-conditioning and so on) are factored into the price. In certain geographical areas, such as California and the Northeast, median home prices are more than 50 percent above the national average and have far exceeded inflation.

Additional Information

Merrill Lynch Capital Markets, Commerce Department. 155 Broadway, New York, NY 10080.

Housing Costs and Benefits Analysis Program, Cooperative Extension/Consumer Economics and Housing Department, Cornell University. Ithaca, NY 14853.

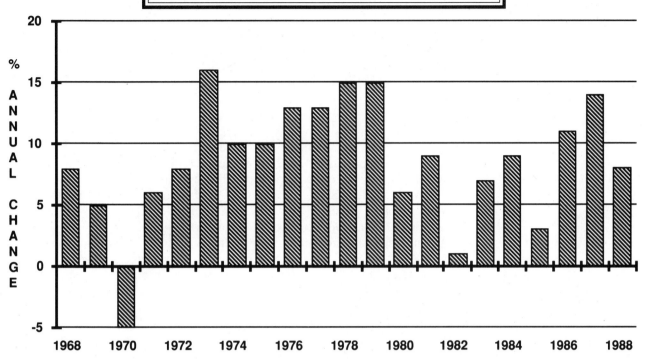

Year	Price	Annual Change	Cumulative Total
1968	$26,600	8%	8%
1969	$27,900	5%	13%
1970	$26,600	-5%	7%
1971	$28,300	6%	13%
1972	$30,500	8%	22%
1973	$35,500	16%	42%
1974	$38,900	10%	56%
1975	$42,600	10%	72%
1976	$48,000	13%	94%
1977	$54,200	13%	119%
1978	$62,500	15%	152%
1979	$71,800	15%	190%
1980	$76,400	6%	207%
1981	$83,000	9%	235%
1982	$83,900	1%	238%
1983	$89,800	7%	262%
1984	$97,600	9%	295%
1985	$100,800	3%	307%
1986	$111,900	11%	352%
1987	$127,200	14%	415%
1988	$137,500	8%	456%

Average compound annual price increase over the last 21 years = 8.5%.

Consumer Price Index (Inflation)

In the United States inflation is tracked by the consumer price index (CPI). The CPI is an index of the retail prices of a "market basket" of consumer goods. The CPI measures changes in consumer prices, as reported by the U.S. Bureau of Labor Statistics each month. The major components of the CPI are housing, food, transportation and energy costs. The CPI is also known as the *cost-of-living index*.

Changes in the inflation rate have had very predictable effects on stock market returns. The highest returns over the past two centuries occurred in the years of rapid price deceleration. Real returns, meaning returns adjusted for inflation, were lowest in periods when inflation was rapidly increasing.

After World War II, price controls were removed in the United States and the cost of goods and services soared. In 1946 inflation was 18 percent, the highest it has ever been except during the Revolutionary and Civil wars. The inflation rate dropped quickly over the next five years, and from 1951 to 1965 it ranged from one-half percent to three percent. The compound annual inflation rate over these 14 years was less than 1.5 percent. During this same period of time, inflation was heating up around the rest of the world.

In 1966 U.S. inflation rates began rising steadily. The CPI hit 5.4 percent in 1969 and peaked at 11 percent in 1974. Inflation reached a post-1950 high of 13 percent in 1980. By the end of 1981, the CPI stood at triple its 1965 level. In 1982 inflation rates began to drop dramatically. In the mid-1980s the CPI approached the levels of the 1952–1965 period. These lower figures were largely due to a decrease in energy prices worldwide.

Inflation affects the returns on various assets differently. Some asset categories, such as rare United States coins and stamps, real estate, gold, metals funds, and oil, prosper during inflationary periods. Other investments, such as money market funds, gold, silver, and platinum, keep up with inflation; and still other assets, such as bonds, GNMAs, bank certificates of deposit, and savings accounts, lose real value during periods of inflation.

Almost all categories of equities and bonds lose real value during inflationary times. The longer the term of the bond, the more paper loss investors will experience in real terms. Money market accounts and short-term CDs are simply hedges against inflation, but often only on a pretax basis. Metals funds and real estate can show very high real returns when inflation is accelerating. This is even more likely with silver than with gold bullion.

Additional Information

Bureau of Economic Analysis, U.S. Department of Commerce. Tower Building, Washington, DC 20230. (202) 523-0777.

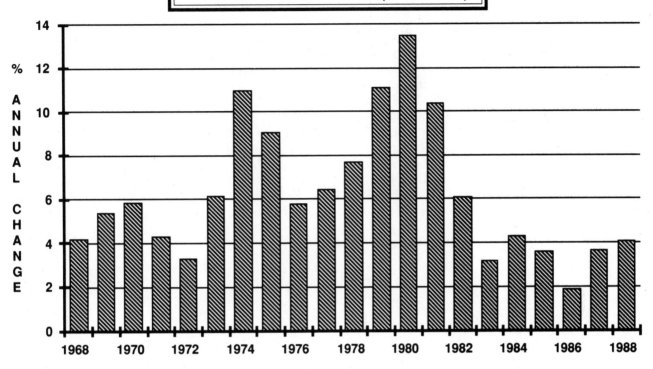

Year	Annual Change	Cumulative Total
1968	4.2%	4%
1969	5.4%	9%
1970	5.9%	16%
1971	4.3%	21%
1972	3.3%	25%
1973	6.2%	33%
1974	11.0%	48%
1975	9.1%	61%
1976	5.8%	71%
1977	6.5%	83%
1978	7.7%	98%
1979	11.1%	120%
1980	13.5%	151%
1981	10.4%	176%
1982	6.1%	193%
1983	3.2%	202%
1984	4.3%	214%
1985	3.6%	227%
1986	1.9%	234%
1987	3.7%	247%
1988	4.1%	261%

Average compound annual rate of inflation for the last 21 years = 6.3%.

Producer Price Index

The producer price index (PPI) measures the change in *wholesale* prices and is formally called the *wholesale price index*. The producer price index measures average changes in prices received by domestic producers of commodities in all stages of processing; imports are not included.

Most of the information used in calculating the PPI is obtained through a sampling of most industries in the manufacturing and mining sectors of the economy. The PPI is based on selling prices reported by establishments of all sizes. The sample currently contains about 3,100 commodities and 75,000 price quotations per month.

The figures used by the producer price index are released monthly by the U.S. Bureau of Labor Statistics. The PPI is usually released on the first or second Friday of each month for the preceding month.

Additional Information

Department of Labor, Bureau of Labor Statistics. 600 E Street, NW, Washington, DC 20212. (202) 272-5113.

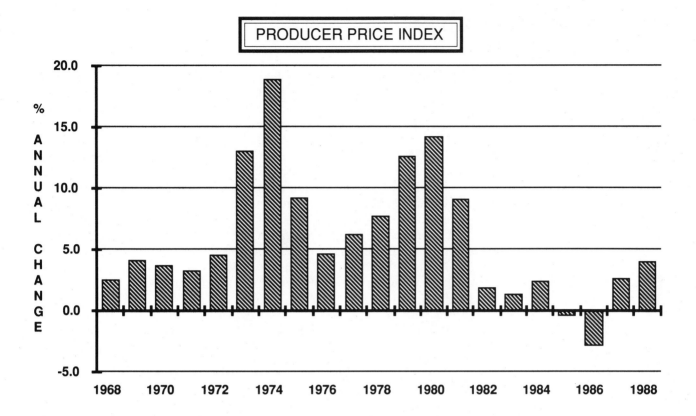

PRODUCER PRICE INDEX

Year	Index	Annual Change	Cumulative Total
1968	34.2	2.5%	3%
1969	35.6	4.1%	7%
1970	36.9	3.7%	11%
1971	38.1	3.3%	14%
1972	39.8	4.5%	20%
1973	45.0	13.1%	36%
1974	53.5	18.9%	62%
1975	58.4	9.2%	77%
1976	61.1	4.6%	86%
1977	64.9	6.2%	97%
1978	69.9	7.7%	113%
1979	78.7	12.6%	141%
1980	89.9	14.2%	175%
1981	98.1	9.1%	200%
1982	100.0	1.9%	206%
1983	101.3	1.3%	209%
1984	103.7	2.4%	215%
1985	103.2	-0.5%	212%
1986	100.2	-2.9%	203%
1987	102.8	2.6%	212%
1988	106.9	4.0%	224%

Average annual increase for the last 21 years = 5.8%.

Gross National Product

The GNP represents the value of all goods and services produced in an economy over a particular period of time, usually one year. The GNP growth rate is perhaps the major indicator as to how an economy is performing. GNP is made up of consumer and government purchases, domestic and foreign investments in the country and the total value of exports.

The GNP of the United States, which is shown on the next chart and graph, represents almost one-fourth of the entire world's GNP. The GNP of the United States represents close to one-third of the entire free world's GNP. The United States is ranked sixth worldwide in per capita income; Sweden is ranked first.

One important use of a country's GNP is to measure its deficit in proper terms. In the United States our current deficit, when taken as a percentage of GNP, is at the same level as it was in 1964. In fact, it is currently *lower* than it was during the whole period of 1940 through 1964. By historical standards, current deficit levels as a percentage of GNP are not at all unusual, or even particularly high.

The GNP is a measure of the ability of an economy to pay off its national debt. As an analogy, suppose a borrower took out a loan for $10,000 while only earning $1,000 a year. The borrower would never be able to pay off the loan. However, a borrower who earned $100,000 a year would have no difficulty in paying it off. Our economy is the same way.

Consumer demand plays an integral role in fueling a country's GNP. Consumers are less likely to consume goods and services if they have less to spend. In contrast, the economy, so the argument goes, picks up speed when taxpayers have more to spend. This argument does not carry a great deal of weight when income tax receipts over the past 50 years are examined.

Federal revenue from taxes on individual income is close to eight percent of GNP, down from almost ten percent in 1981. This 1981 level of income tax revenues was last matched in 1944. Over the past 40 years, the level of personal income taxes as a percentage of GNP has had a narrow range — from six to ten percent.

It has been argued that our high levels of private debt may deter economic activity due to lower net income after debt servicing. Total U.S. consumer and corporate debt equalled 124 percent of GNP in 1987; the level of private debt has ranged between 97 and 124 percent of GNP over the past 25 years. Surprisingly, Japanese and West German corporations are far more leveraged than their American counterparts.

Additional Information

Economics Department, Manufacturers Hanover Trust Company. 270 Park Avenue, New York, NY 10017. (212) 286-7351.

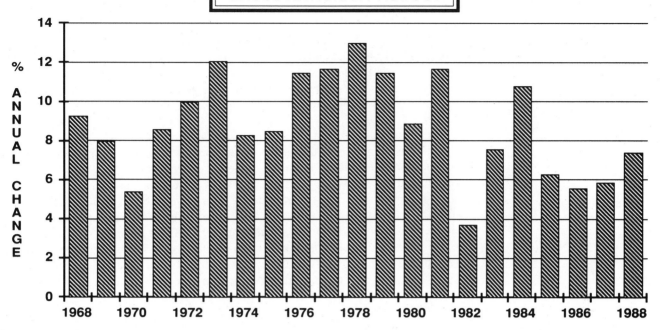

Year	GNP	Annual Change	Cumulative Total
1968	892.7	9.3%	9%
1969	963.9	8.0%	18%
1970	1,015.5	5.4%	35%
1972	1,212.8	10.0%	49%
1973	1,359.3	12.1%	67%
1974	1,472.8	8.3%	80%
1975	1,598.4	8.5%	96%
1976	1,782.8	11.5%	120%
1977	1,990.5	11.7%	146%
1978	2,249.5	13.0%	178%
1979	2,508.2	11.5%	211%
1980	2,732.0	8.9%	239%
1981	3,052.6	11.7%	280%
1982	3,166.0	3.7%	295%
1983	3,405.7	7.6%	327%
1984	3,772.2	10.8%	374%
1985	4,010.3	6.3%	402%
1986	4,235.0	5.6%	432%
1987	4,486.2	5.9%	464%
1988	4,818.2	7.4%	503%*

Average GNP growth for the last 21 years = 8.9%.

* preliminary

Standard and Poor's 500 Dividend Yield

Dividend yields are highest during periods of low stock prices. Yields peaked in the early 1940s and early 1950s; the highest was 8.3 percent in 1950. The lowest dividend yields occurred in the boom periods of the late 1920s, 1960s and early 1970s. The lowest was 2.95 percent in 1972. The height of the bull market in 1987 also saw average dividend yields of less than three percent.

Yields are high when prices are low because dividend payments are less volatile and more controllable than stock prices. When stock prices drop, corporate officers often maintain dividends to sustain investor confidence, driving up the dividend yield. Despite this correlation, a stock's dividend yield has not had a direct relation to its return over the last 20 years.

The table and graph on the following page depict the average common dividend yield of U.S. stocks, as measured by the S&P 500.

The stock dividend yields of foreign indexes as of 1988 were: 3.9 percent (Australia), 3.1 percent (Canada), 1.8 percent (Europe, Australia, Far East [EAFE] Index), 3.4 percent (France), 4.1 percent (West Germany), 4.2 percent (Hong Kong), 3.0 percent (Italy), .5 percent (Japan), 3.3 percent (Spain), 2.5 percent (Switzerland), 4.7 percent (United Kingdom), and 2.5 percent for the entire world.

This book includes a number of S&P 500–related charts because this index is more representative of the stock market than the Dow Jones Industrial Average (DJIA). The S&P 500 includes far more issues and is computed based on the value (importance) of each individual issue. For these two reasons, the ratings of most money managers are based on their performance against the S&P, not the Dow.

Additional Information

Standard and Poor's Corporation. 25 Broadway, New York, NY 10004. (212) 208-8690.

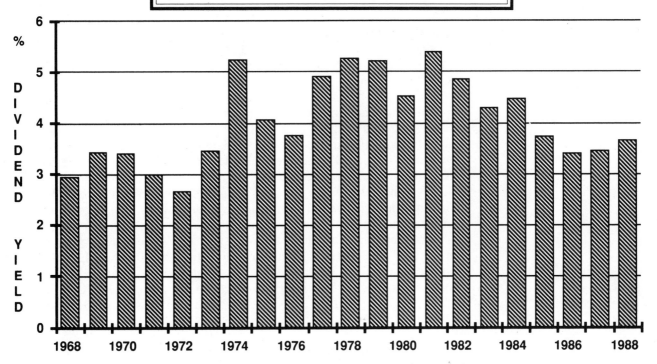

Year	Average Dividend Yield	Cumulative Total
1968	2.96%	3%
1969	3.43%	6%
1970	3.41%	9%
1971	3.01%	12%
1972	2.67%	15%
1973	3.46%	18%
1974	5.25%	24%
1975	4.08%	29%
1976	3.77%	34%
1977	4.91%	41%
1978	5.28%	48%
1979	5.23%	55%
1980	4.54%	63%
1981	5.41%	71%
1982	4.88%	80%
1983	4.30%	87%
1984	4.50%	96%
1985	3.74%	104%
1986	3.42%	110%
1987	3.47%	116%
1988	3.68%	125%

Average dividend for the last 21 years = 4.07%.

Standard and Poor's 500 Year-End P/E Ratio

The price-earnings (P/E) ratio is the price of a stock divided by its earnings per share. The price-earnings ratio, also known as the *multiple*, gives investors a means of determining if they might be paying too much for the stock. A high P/E ratio for the S&P 500 could signal that the market is currently overvalued and possibly should be avoided.

The price-earnings ratio is a commonly used statistic for assessing stock values across business sectors and between companies. Generally, low P/E ratios prevail during periods of low stock prices. In 15 of the past 60 years, the market's average P/E ratio fell below ten. After a period of low P/E ratios, the market has often rallied sharply.

Over the past 20 years, studies have shown that P/E ratios have had a direct relationship to return. In general, buying stocks with low P/E ratios has been, and may continue to be, a profitable strategy.

The graph and table on the following page depict the price-earnings ratio of the U.S. stock market, as measured by the S&P 500. The P/E ratios for other countries as of 1988 were: 12.6 (Australia), 12.4 (Canada), 24.9 (Europe, Australia, Far East [EAFE] Index), 10.9 (France), 13.5 (Germany), 12.1 (Hong Kong), 13.1 (Italy), 57.5 (Japan), 18.4 (Spain), 13.1 (Switzerland), 12.0 (United Kingdom), and 19.1 for the entire world.

Additional Information

Fortune. 1271 Avenue of the Americas, New York, NY 10020. (212) 586-1212.

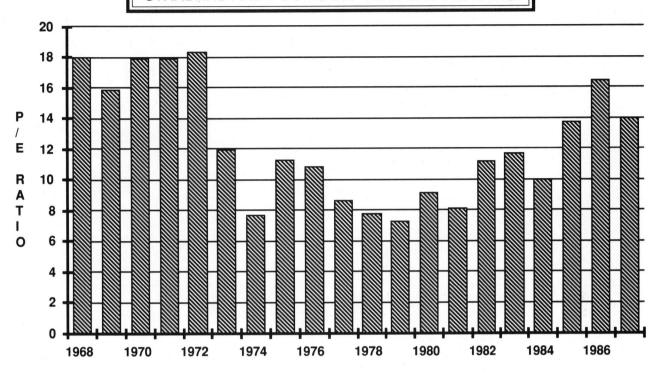

STANDARD AND POOR'S 500 YEAR-END P/E RATIO

Year	Average P/E Ratio	Change
1968	18.03	-0.4%
1969	15.93	-11.7%
1970	17.96	12.7%
1971	17.91	-0.3%
1972	18.39	2.7%
1973	11.95	-35.0%
1974	7.71	-35.5%
1975	11.33	47.0%
1976	10.84	-4.3%
1977	8.70	-19.7%
1978	7.79	-10.5%
1979	7.25	-6.9%
1980	9.19	26.8%
1981	8.12	-11.6%
1982	11.20	37.9%
1983	11.73	4.7%
1984	10.00	-14.8%
1985	13.79	37.9%
1986	16.52	19.8%
1987	14.03	-15.1%

Average P/E ratio for the last 20 years = 12.4%

MUTUAL FUNDS

All Funds

Approximately 1,300 mutual funds represent "all funds." The average annual expense rate of all mutual funds, excluding money market funds, is 1.20 percent of the assets being managed. The figures shown in the accompanying graph and table are net of all ongoing costs and expenses.

The *all funds* category includes all types of mutual funds except money market funds. Counting the nearly 1,000 different money market funds, there are now more mutual funds than stocks listed on the NYSE.

Mutual funds are further classified by either being *full load, low load, back-end load* (also known as *12b-1 funds*) and *no-load*. The term *load* simply means commission or charge. Thus, all of the aforementioned classifications, except no load, charge a sales commission either directly or indirectly to the investor.

Funds categorized as full load have a sliding-scale commission rate that can be as high as 8.5 percent. The more the investor puts into a fund family, the lower the sales commission charge. The fee can drop to as low as 0.3 percent. Full load *bond* funds usually start out at a 4.75 percent commission charge for investments under $50,000 and then match the schedule used by equity funds for investments of $50,000 or greater.

Low-load funds have become quite popular during the last few years. Most full-load funds are reducing their sales charges, while many no-load funds are beginning to charge low loads. One of the most commonly used sales charge schedules used for low-load funds starts at a 4.75 percent commission and declines for cumulative purchases of $50,000 or more.

A 12b-1 fund, also known as a *back-end load fund*, does not charge the investor an initial commission; 100 percent of the invested amount goes to work for the investor. However, a 12b-1 fund charges an additional annual fee that normally ranges from .75 percent to 1.25 percent. Because the investor did not pay a direct commission up-front, a penalty is imposed on principal withdrawals during a scheduled period.

The back-end penalty is between two percent and six percent. Some 12b-1 funds have a declining sales charge that is reduced by one percent each year. Thus, a fund with an initial four percent deferred sales charge would only charge one percent at the end of three years, disappearing altogether by the end of the fourth year. Other funds have deferred charges, also known as *penalties*, that stay level for a specific period, usually four to six years, and then drop off to no penalty. All 12b-1 funds allow investors to take out dividends, interest and growth anytime without charge.

No-load funds do not charge the investor a sales commission. Whereas funds that charge a commission are largely promoted by the brokerage community, no-load funds are publicized by advertising campaigns such as mailers, television commercials and ads in magazines and newspapers. In order to pay for such promotions, no-load funds have to increase their expenses. Such expenses are passed on to existing fund shareholders. Increased expenses translate into reduced returns for investors. Fortunately, these increased expenses frequently translate into costs that average less than one percent extra per year.

There is a great deal of controversy as to whether investors should pay a commission charge when purchasing a mutual fund. The decision is not as simple as saying that one group always outperforms the other. Nevertheless, all other items being equal, investors should avoid funds that impose a sales charge if their intent is to stay within the fund family for a short period.

For anticipated holding periods exceeding six to eight years, 12b-1 funds should not be used. The additional 12b-1 fee levied against investors each year makes this group of funds more and more expensive to own as time goes on.

The decision whether to purchase a fund that charges any type of commission should depend on the service and the expertise being offered by the investment counselor. Some investors are better off doing their own research and ongoing review. Others will find comfort in dealing with a brokerage firm or financial planner who has knowledge in this area. Selecting mutual funds is much more difficult than simply picking the top performers. Unfortunately, most investors and brokers still do not realize this fact.

The accompanying table and graph represent how investors would have fared had they placed an equal amount of money in each one of the eight major fund categories (aggressive growth, balanced, bond and preferred, growth, growth and income, international, metals, and municipal bonds).

Additional Information

Mutual Fund Values. c/o Morningstar, Inc., 53 West Jackson Boulevard, Chicago, IL 60604. (800) 876-5005.

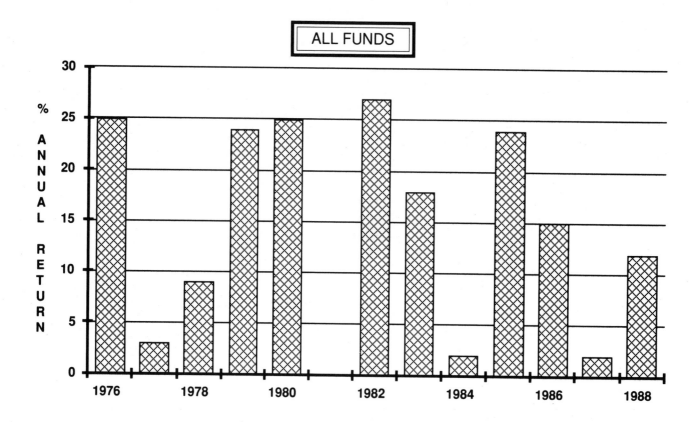

Year	Annual Return	Cumulative Total
1976	25%	25%
1977	3%	29%
1978	9%	41%
1979	24%	75%
1980	25%	119%
1981	0%	119%
1982	27%	178%
1983	18%	228%
1984	2%	235%
1985	24%	315%
1986	15%	377%
1987	2%	387%
1988	12%	445%

Average compound annual return for the last 13 years = 13.9%.

Aggressive Growth Funds

An aggressive growth mutual fund looks for stocks that are poised for fast growth. Funds of this nature may use high-risk techniques, such as short-selling, leverage, high turnover, options and futures contracts. Approximately 55 funds comprise this category. The volatility of this group, on average, is almost 20 percent greater than the market as a whole. At 1.4 percent of total assets, aggressive growth funds also have one of the highest average annual expense rates. The figures shown in the accompanying graph and table are net of all ongoing costs and expenses.

The objective of aggressive growth funds is maximum gain. They tend to invest in common stocks of small companies and stay fully invested during good and bad market periods. Normally, these funds pay a very small cash dividend.

Many aggressive growth funds concentrate their assets in particular industries or segments of the market. Such segmentation reduces overall diversification and increases risk. Thus, this group tends to outperform the overall market during bull markets, but fares worse during bear markets.

Generally, long-term investors who are not concerned with monthly or yearly variations in investment return should be highly rewarded. Due to the extreme variance of return found with aggressive funds, risk-averse investors, or those with a short-term investment horizon, may find that this group is outside their comfort zone.

Additional Information

Investment Company Institute. 1600 M Street, Washington, DC 20036. (202) 293-7700.

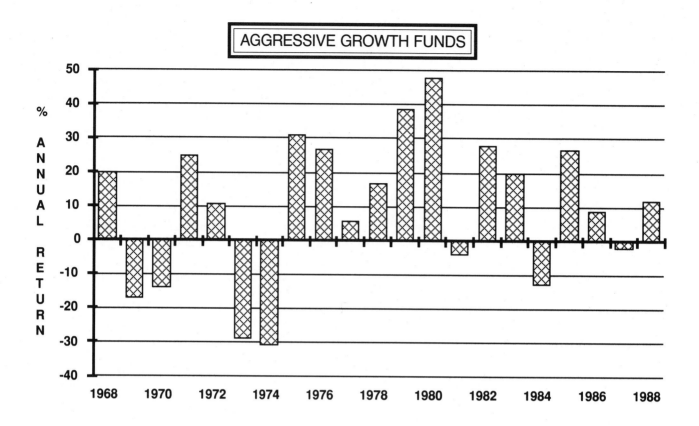

Year	Annual Return	Cumulative Total
1968	20%	20%
1969	-17%	0%
1970	-14%	-14%
1971	25%	8%
1972	11%	20%
1973	-29%	-15%
1974	-31%	-41%
1975	31%	-23%
1976	27%	-2%
1977	6%	4%
1978	17%	22%
1979	39%	70%
1980	48%	152%
1981	-4%	142%
1982	28%	210%
1983	20%	272%
1984	-13%	224%
1985	27%	311%
1986	9%	348%
1987	-2%	339%
1988	12%	392%

Average compound annual return for the last 21 years = 7.9%.

Balanced Funds

Balanced funds, also known as *total return* funds, invest in both stocks and bonds. The name for this group of mutual funds is based on its investment objective—somewhat of a balance between stocks and bonds. A fund manager of a balanced fund has the flexibility of being able to favor stocks over bonds or vice versa.

Over 60 funds constitute this category. The percentage range of equities and debt instruments that will be held is stated in each fund's prospectus. The volatility of this group is slightly more than half that of the stock market, giving it an overall risk level somewhere between low and moderate. The average annual expense rate of balanced funds is almost 1.20 percent of assets managed. The figures shown in the accompanying graph and table are net of all ongoing costs and expenses.

As a result of their investment objectives, balanced funds provide a high dividend and interest yield. Due to the comparatively large payout stream of balanced funds, people in moderate and high income-tax brackets should consider using tax-sheltered money for this type of investment.

Additional Information

Institute for Econometric Research. 3471 North Federal Highway, Fort Lauderdale, FL 33306. (800) 327-6720.

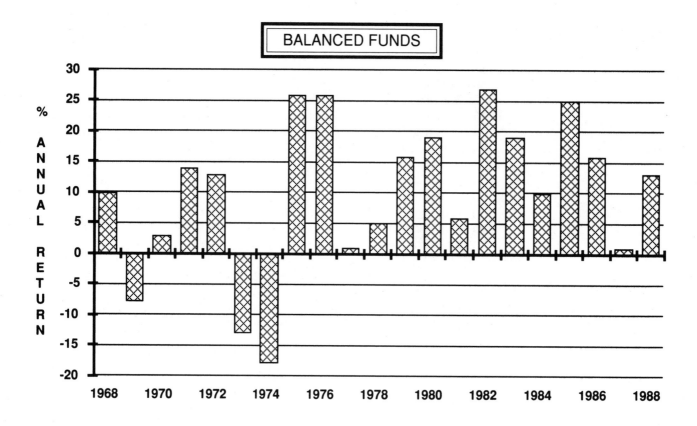

Year	Annual Return	Cumulative Total
1968	10%	10%
1969	-8%	1%
1970	3%	4%
1971	14%	19%
1972	13%	34%
1973	-13%	17%
1974	-18%	-4%
1975	26%	21%
1976	26%	52%
1977	1%	54%
1978	5%	62%
1979	16%	88%
1980	19%	124%
1981	6%	137%
1982	27%	201%
1983	19%	258%
1984	10%	294%
1985	25%	393%
1986	16%	472%
1987	1%	478%
1988	13%	553%

Average compound annual return for the last 21 years = 9.3%.

Bond and Preferred Funds

Bond and preferred funds invest in fixed-income securities of various quality ratings and maturities. In light of their objectives, most of these funds are comprised of safe debt instruments; an average maturity of over 20 years helps increase the current yield. Other funds within this category have short-term or medium-term maturing instruments, resulting in yields of one to two percent less but obtaining greater price stability. Often the title of the fund will indicate its major trait. Normally, these funds invest in securities of the United States. Only a handful of funds invest in foreign bonds.

Some bond funds specialize in municipal issues; others invest in only U.S. government bonds or agency issues, such as Ginnie Maes. Still others invest in corporate debt. High-yield, also known as *junk*, bond funds invest in lower-rated corporate or municipal securities.

Preferred funds are comprised of bonds, convertibles, common stocks and preferred stocks. Preferred stocks are equity instruments that normally have a stated rate of return, similar to bonds. Even though preferreds are stocks, they act more like bonds. Preferreds are most sensitive to interest-rate movements. Increased corporate earnings or a rally in the underlying common stock may have little or no effect on the price per share of a preferred. There are less than a dozen preferred mutual funds.

Over 230 funds comprise the bond and preferred fund group. There is only an approximate ten percent correlation between this category of funds and the overall stock market. The average annual expense rate of these funds is slightly over one percent of all assets managed. The figures shown in the accompanying graph and table are net of all ongoing costs and expenses.

Additional Information

Wiesenberger's Investment Company Service. c/o Warren, Gorham and Lamont, 1633 Broadway, New York, NY 10019. (800) 922-0066.

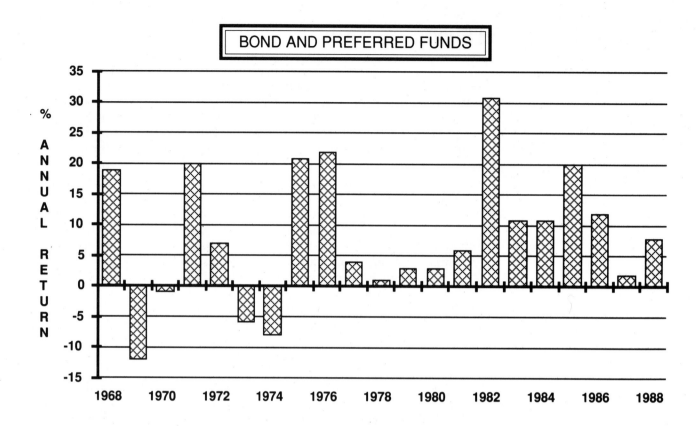

Year	Annual Return	Cumulative Total
1968	19%	19%
1969	-12%	5%
1970	-1%	4%
1971	20%	25%
1972	7%	34%
1973	-6%	26%
1974	-8%	16%
1975	21%	40%
1976	22%	71%
1977	4%	78%
1978	1%	80%
1979	3%	85%
1980	3%	91%
1981	6%	102%
1982	31%	165%
1983	11%	194%
1984	11%	226%
1985	20%	291%
1986	12%	338%
1987	2%	347%
1988	8%	383%

Average compound annual return for the last 21 years = 7.8%.

Growth Funds

A growth fund's primary objective is growth of capital. Approximately 290 funds comprise this category. These funds concentrate in companies whose earnings are expected to grow faster than average. Concern about current income, if at all, is a distant second.

The volatility of these funds is slightly less than the overall stock market. Unlike aggressive growth funds, growth funds generally do not engage in speculative tactics such as using borrowed monies or selling stocks short (betting a security will drop in value). On an infrequent basis, these funds will use stock or index options to *reduce* risk by hedging existing security positions.

Growth funds typically are more stable than aggressive growth funds. They invest in firms that are older, larger and pay larger cash dividends. Companies such as GE, Merck and GM are common in the portfolios of growth funds. The amount of diversification is also greater in growth than in aggressive funds. Less concentration in a given industry or security is another reason why this group does not have the volatility common with aggressive growth funds.

The overall average annual expense of these funds is approximately 1.25 percent of assets. The figures shown in the accompanying graph and table are net of all ongoing costs and expenses.

Additional Information

Investment Information Services. 205 West Wacker Drive, Chicago, IL 60606.
(312) 750-9300.

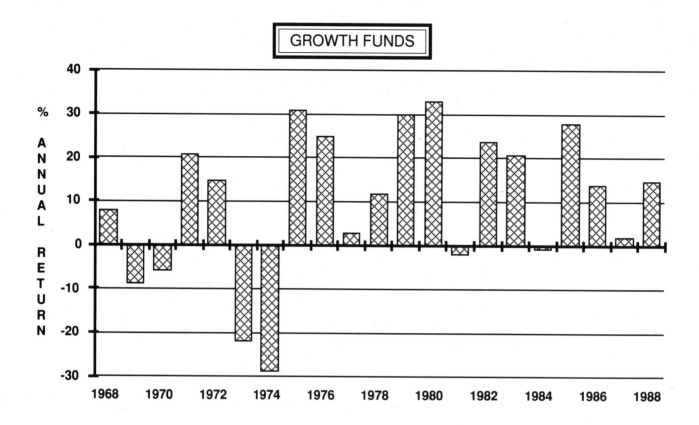

Year	Annual Return	Cumulative Total
1968	8%	8%
1969	-9%	-2%
1970	-6%	-8%
1971	21%	11%
1972	15%	28%
1973	-22%	0%
1974	-29%	-29%
1975	31%	-7%
1976	25%	16%
1977	3%	19%
1978	12%	33%
1979	30%	73%
1980	33%	130%
1981	-2%	125%
1982	24%	179%
1983	21%	238%
1984	-1%	235%
1985	28%	329%
1986	14%	389%
1987	2%	399%
1988	15%	474%

Average compound annual return for the last 21 years = 8.7%.

Growth and Income Funds

Growth and income mutual funds seek growth of capital and current income as almost equal objectives. Over 150 funds comprise the growth and income category. These funds invest in equities and convertibles. They have a market volatility that is only 75 percent as great as the S&P 500.

Growth and income funds generally invest in well-established companies that have a long history of paying cash dividends. The funds try to provide their shareholders with comparatively high dividend income, along with long-term growth. They generally avoid securities of companies that would cause the fund to experience considerable changes in its net asset value. The standard deviation of this group of funds is approximately 16, making them almost 20 percent less volatile than growth funds.

Because of the relatively high current income offered by these kinds of funds, often in the five to six percent range, prospective investors should note that distributions from these funds are fully taxable in the year in which they are paid or reinvested. All mutual funds are required to distribute dividends and capital gains at least once a year.

The average annual expense rate of these funds is close to 1.20 percent of all assets managed. The figures shown in the accompanying graph and table are net of all ongoing costs and expenses.

Additional Information

Mutual Fund Services. The OLDE Building, 735 Griswold Street, Detroit, MI 48226. (800) 225-FUND.

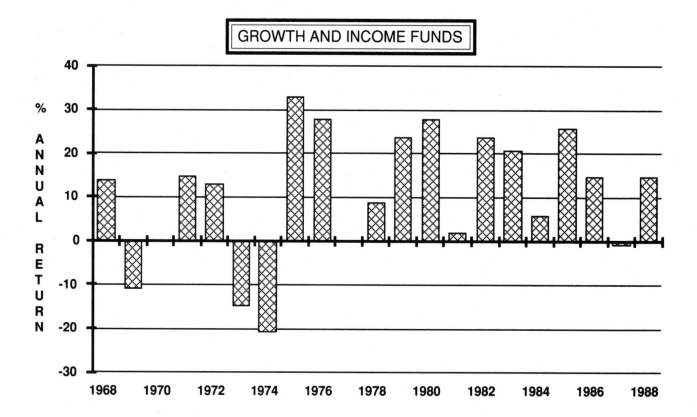

Year	Annual Return	Cumulative Total
1968	14%	14%
1969	-11%	1%
1970	0%	1%
1971	15%	16%
1972	13%	31%
1973	-15%	11%
1974	-21%	-12%
1975	33%	17%
1976	28%	50%
1977	0%	50%
1978	9%	64%
1979	24%	103%
1980	28%	160%
1981	2%	165%
1982	24%	229%
1983	21%	298%
1984	6%	322%
1985	26%	432%
1986	15%	512%
1987	-1%	506%
1988	15%	597%

Average compound annual return for the last 21 years = 9.7%.

International Mutual Funds

International mutual funds invest primarily in foreign equity securities. Some funds specialize in regions, such as the Pacific or Europe; others invest worldwide. In addition, some funds, usually termed *global*, invest in both foreign and U.S. stocks.

Foreign funds provide investors with added diversification. The most important factor when diversifying a portfolio is selecting assets that do not behave similarly under a given economic scenario. The more independently a foreign market moves in relation to the U.S. market, the greater its diversification and the lower its risk potential. Several studies have shown that a portfolio comprised of U.S. and foreign stocks has one half the risk level of a similar portfolio comprised only of U.S. equities.

International funds overcome some of the difficulties investors would face in making foreign investments directly. For instance, individuals would have to thoroughly understand the foreign brokerage process, be familiar with the various foreign marketplaces and their economies, be aware of currency fluctuation trends and have access to reliable financial information.

These points should be considered when investing internationally. In addition to the risk inherent in investing in any security, there is an additional exchange rate, or currency, risk. The return to a U.S. investor from a foreign security depends on both the security's return in its own currency, plus the rate at which that currency can be exchanged for U.S. dollars. The currency play can have a dramatic effect on a foreign fund's performance for any given year. However, over a ten-year period, the currency exchange rate has been unimportant.

Roughly 60 mutual funds comprise the international category. There is approximately a 75 percent correlation between international funds and the S&P 500. The average annual expense rate of these funds is almost 1.5 percent of all assets managed, making them the most expensive category of mutual funds to manage. The figures shown in the accompanying graph and table are net of all ongoing costs and expenses.

Additional Information

American Association of Individual Investors. 612 North Michigan Avenue, Chicago, IL 60611. (312) 280-0170.

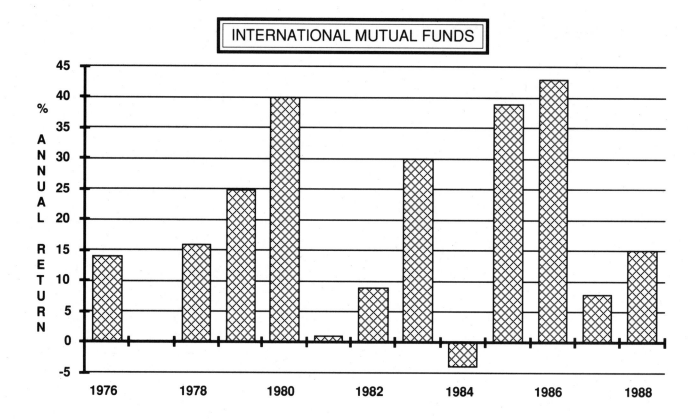

Year	Annual Return	Cumulative Total
1976	14%	14%
1977	0%	14%
1978	16%	32%
1979	25%	65%
1980	40%	131%
1981	1%	133%
1982	9%	154%
1983	30%	230%
1984	-4%	217%
1985	39%	341%
1986	43%	531%
1987	8%	581%
1988	15%	683%

Average compound annual return for the last 13 years = 17.2%.

Metals Funds

Metals mutual funds, also referred to as *gold mutual funds*, specialize in investments in both foreign and domestic companies that mine gold and other precious metals. These types of funds are also part of a special category known as *sector* or *specialty* funds, which concentrate their investments in one economic or geographic area.

The appeal of gold and other metals is that they have performed well during extremely inflationary periods. Over the short term, the price of these metals moves in response to a variety of political, economic and psychological forces. Because gold, silver and platinum tend to perform in an inverse relationship to stocks, bonds and cash, metals can be used as a stabilizing component in one's portfolio.

Precious metals funds, like the metals themselves, are very volatile, often shooting from the bottom to the top and back to the bottom in fund rankings over the years. Investors should understand, however, that because most gold funds invest in the stock of gold mining companies, gold funds are still subject to some stock market influences.

Over the long term, most gold investors have only broken even on an after-inflation basis. In general, gold's price fluctuates wildly, but this asset does provide portfolio diversification and a hedge against inflation. The standard deviation of metals funds is 50 percent greater than the variation of returns for gold bullion. Silver, the second-most-important monetary metal, is traded in a much smaller market than gold, and its prices are even more volatile.

There are almost 25 metals funds. This classification of funds has slightly less than a 60 percent correlation with the overall stock market. The average annual expense rate of these funds is approximately 1.3 percent of all assets managed. The figures shown in the accompanying graph and table are net of all ongoing costs and expenses.

Additional Information

CDA Investment Technologies. 1355 Piccard Drive, Rockville, MD 20850. (301) 590-1311.

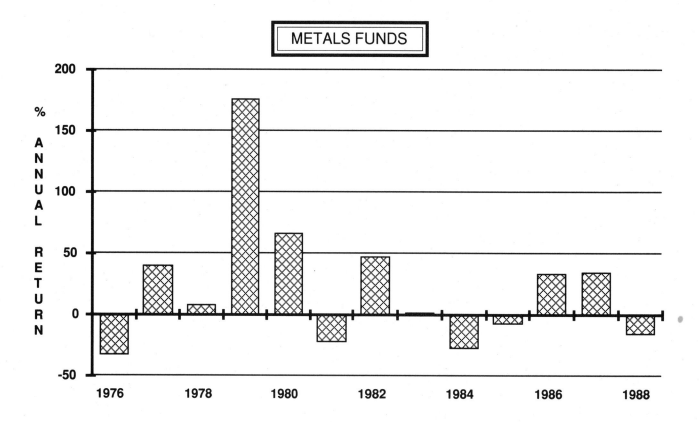

Year	Annual Return	Cumulative Total
1976	-33%	-33%
1977	40%	-6%
1978	8%	2%
1979	176%	182%
1980	67%	371%
1981	-23%	263%
1982	48%	437%
1983	2%	448%
1984	-28%	295%
1985	-8%	263%
1986	34%	386%
1987	35%	556%
1988	-16%	451%

Average compound annual return for the last 13 years = 14.0%.

Money Market Funds

Money market funds are open-ended mutual funds that invest in commercial paper, short-term government securities, CDs and other highly liquid and safe securities that pay interest. The average maturity of these instruments ranges from 25 to 60 days. Launched in 1975, these funds are especially popular during inflationary periods and stock market declines.

Fees to run a money market fund are well under one percent of the assets managed. Interest rates or yields quoted to investors are net of any and all fees. The fund's net asset value (NAV) always remains at one dollar per share. It is only the interest rate paid by the fund that changes. If interest rates go up, the rate earned in a money market fund also increases and vice versa. Such funds often offer free check-writing privileges.

Money market funds have a perfect track record: None have ever lost any money. The interest thrown off from most of these funds is fully taxable. Some funds, comprised of federal obligations only, may be exempt from state income tax. Still others, commonly referred to as *tax-free money market funds*, are exempt from federal and state income taxes. Tax-free money market funds have rates that equal approximately 65 percent of the pretax yields offered by regular money market accounts. Many money market funds are part of a fund family. This means investors can switch their money from one fund to another and back again without additional charge.

Money market funds, bank CDs and T-bills have very small standard deviations. This means that this small handful of investment vehicles comprise about the only havens where investors may go without experiencing moderate or large swings in the value of their principal. In the case of money market funds, an investor cannot lose money due to interest rate swings or penalties.

Investors' attitudes toward money market instruments have changed over the last dozen years. Money market accounts were once considered only a temporary parking place for monies, until they could be invested in other assets. Since the mid-1970s, with high rates of inflation, cash equivalents have become a more prominent investment vehicle, with returns that often exceed inflation on a pretax basis.

Additional Information

The Donoghue Organization. 360 Woodland Street, P.O. Box 540, Holliston, MA 01746. (800) 343-5413.

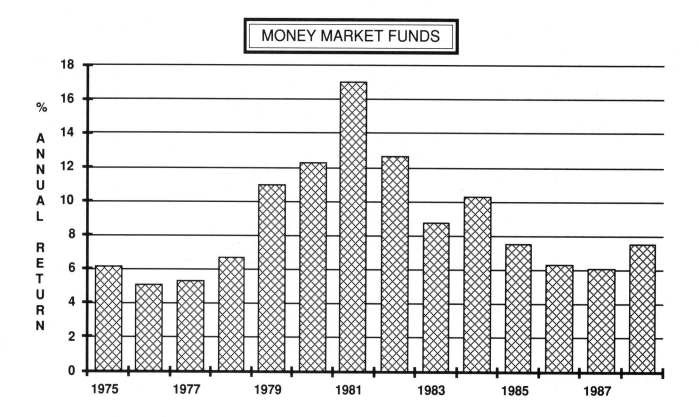

Year	Average Annual Return	Cumulative Total
1975	6.2%	6%
1976	5.1%	11%
1977	5.3%	17%
1978	6.7%	25%
1979	11.0%	39%
1980	12.3%	56%
1981	17.1%	83%
1982	12.7%	107%
1983	8.8%	126%
1984	10.3%	149%
1985	7.6%	169%
1986	6.3%	185%
1987	6.1%	202%
1988	7.6%	226%

Average compound annual return for the last 14 years = 8.8%.

Municipal Bond Funds

Municipal bond funds, also known as *tax-free funds*, are comprised of tax-free debt instruments issued by states, counties, districts or political sub-divisions. Interest from municipal bonds is normally exempt from federal income tax. In almost all states, interest is also exempt from state and local income taxes if the portfolio is comprised of issues from the investor's state of residence, a U.S. territory (Puerto Rico, the Virgin Islands, and so on), or the District of Columbia.

Until the early 1980s municipal bonds were almost as sensitive to interest-rate changes as corporate and government bonds. During the last few years, however, tax-free bond funds have taken on a new personality. Now, when interest rates change, municipal bonds exhibit only one half to one third the price change that occurs with similar funds comprised of corporate or government issues. This decreased volatility is due to a smaller supply of municipal bonds and the elimination of almost all tax shelters, which have increased the popularity of tax-free bonds.

Additional Information

Gabriele, Hueglin and Cashman. 44 Wall Street, New York, NY 10005. (800) 422-7435.

The Bond Buyer. One State Street Plaza, New York, NY 10004. (212) 943-8200.

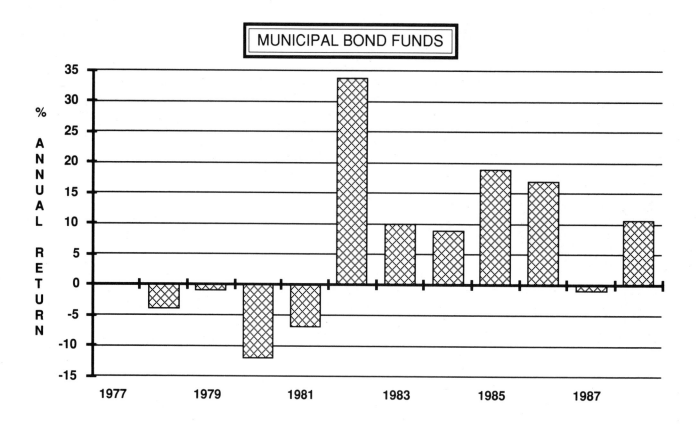

Year	Annual Return	Cumulative Total
1977	0%	0%
1978	-4%	-4%
1979	-1%	-5%
1980	-12%	-16%
1981	-7%	-22%
1982	34%	5%
1983	10%	16%
1984	9%	26%
1985	19%	50%
1986	17%	76%
1987	-1%	74%
1988	11%	93%

Average compound annual return for the last 12 years = 5.6%.

STOCKS

New York Stock Exchange Composite Index

The NYSE Composite Index is a market-value-weighted index that includes all stocks traded on the New York Stock Exchange (NYSE). The NYSE had its slowest day in 1830, when only 31 shares traded. Less than sixty years later, the exchange experienced its first one-million-share day. And in 1982 the NYSE saw its first 100-million-share day. The New York Stock Exchange, also known as the *Big Board*, is the oldest (1792) and largest stock exchange in the United States, located at 11 Wall Street in New York City.

In May 1792 a group of security brokers met under a buttonwood tree and set forth the first commission schedule for what would soon be referred to as *NYSE stocks*. The size of membership (number of seats) was also fixed at this time. From 1792 until 1975 the NYSE was legally regarded as a private club and was permitted monopoly power over security trades. In the mid-1970s the SEC abolished the fixed-commission system, which opened the door for discount brokers.

Total voting membership for the NYSE is currently fixed at 1366 seats, which are owned by individuals who are usually partners or officers of securities firms. The price of a seat has varied quite a bit over the last 20 years. Currently a seat sells for approximately $750,000. More than 500 brokerage firms own seats. Most members execute orders for the public. A small number of traders deal exclusively for their own accounts.

More than 2,300 companies are listed on the NYSE, representing large firms that can meet the exchange's tough listing requirements. NYSE-listed shares make up approximately 60 percent of the total shares traded on organized national exchanges in the United States. In late 1987 the value of these shares exceeded $2.3 trillion.

The NYSE has had an average annual total return of almost nine percent, including dividends, over its almost-200-year history. The standard deviation for the NYSE composite index is close to 16, almost identical to the variances shown in the entire foreign equity marketplace.

Additional Information

New York Stock Exchange, Publications Department. 11 Wall Street, New York, NY 10005.
(212) 623-3000 or (212) 623-2089.

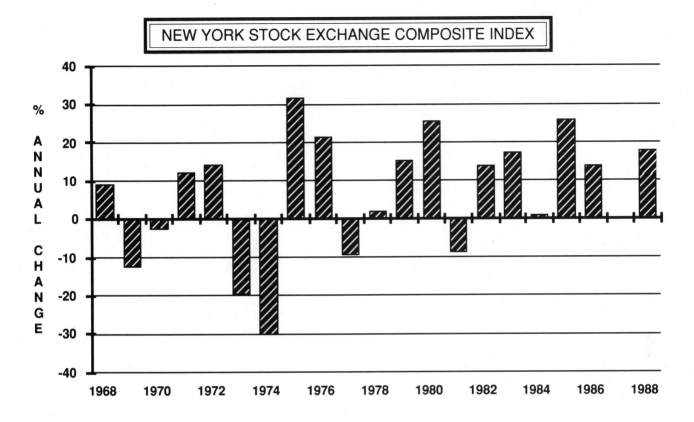

NEW YORK STOCK EXCHANGE COMPOSITE INDEX

Year	Year-End Close	Annual Change	Cumulative Total
1968	58.90	9.4%	9%
1969	51.53	-12.5%	-5%
1970	50.23	-2.5%	-8%
1971	56.43	12.3%	3%
1972	64.48	14.3%	17%
1973	51.82	-19.6%	-6%
1974	36.13	-30.3%	-34%
1975	47.64	31.9%	-13%
1976	57.88	21.5%	5%
1977	52.50	-9.3%	-4%
1978	53.62	2.1%	-2%
1979	61.95	15.5%	14%
1980	77.86	25.7%	44%
1981	71.11	-8.7%	31%
1982	81.03	14.0%	49%
1983	95.18	17.5%	74%
1984	96.38	1.3%	76%
1985	121.58	26.1%	122%
1986	138.58	14.0%	153%
1987	138.23	-0.3%	153%
1988	156.26	18.0%	199%

Average compound annual return for the last 21 years = 5.4% (without dividends reinvested).

American Stock Exchange (AMEX)

A market index of aggregate stock returns shows investors what would happen to monies invested at a particular time, assuming an investment was properly proportioned in relation to each security's weighted value. The American Stock Exchange (AMEX) is such a market index.

The American Stock Exchange has the second-biggest trading volume in the United States. The majority of the stocks and bonds traded on the AMEX are those of small-sized to medium-sized companies, in contrast to the large corporations whose shares are traded on the New York Stock Exchange (NYSE).

The American Stock Exchange is heavily represented by a large number of oil and gas stocks. The AMEX also houses the trading of options on several NYSE and over-the-counter (OTC) stocks. More foreign shares are traded on the AMEX than on any other U.S. exchange. A seat on the AMEX sells for approximately $250,000.

Over 1,300 different issues are listed on the AMEX, with a total 1987 market capitalization of close to $92 billion. Capitalization is calculated by taking the price per share of each issue times the number of shares outstanding.

Additional Information

American Stock Exchange. 86 Trinity Place, New York, NY 10006. (212) 306-1000.

AMERICAN STOCK EXCHANGE (AMEX)

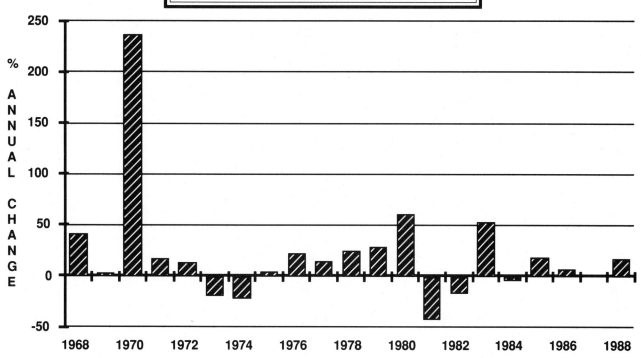

Year	Year-End Close	Annual Change	Cumulative Total
1968	27.72	40.93%	41%
1969	28.73	3.64%	47%
1970	96.63	236.34%	394%
1971	113.40	17.35%	478%
1972	129.10	13.84%	559%
1973	103.80	-19.36%	423%
1974	79.97	-22.96%	311%
1975	83.15	3.98%	327%
1976	101.63	22.22%	421%
1977	116.18	14.32%	494%
1978	144.56	24.43%	637%
1979	186.56	29.05%	851%
1980	300.94	61.31%	1431%
1981	171.79	-42.92%	773%
1982	141.31	-17.74%	616%
1983	216.48	53.20%	995%
1984	207.96	-3.94%	951%
1985	246.13	18.35%	1140%
1986	263.27	6.96%	1227%
1987	260.35	-1.11%	1214%
1988	306.01	17.54%	1451%

Average compound annual return for the last 21 years = 13.9%.

Over-the-Counter Composite

An over-the-counter (OTC) stock is a security that is not listed or traded on an organized exchange. Prospective buyers and sellers contact market makers via telephone or through a computer. Unlike most stocks, which are traded on a particular exchange, usually more than one dealer handles any given OTC security. The National Association of Securities Dealers System (NASDAQ), a computerized system for tracking the performance of over 3,000 OTC stocks, began in 1971. The purpose of NASDAQ is to provide a more orderly method for trading OTC equities.

OTC stocks are traditionally those of smaller companies that do not meet the listing requirements of the NYSE or AMEX. Prices of several thousand OTC stocks are published daily in major newspapers. Quotes for some OTC stocks are only found in the *Pink Sheets*, a publication that comes out weekly.

Over the past 25 years the annualized compound total return for OTC stocks has been close to 12 percent, almost 40 percent greater than the NYSE. There is an extremely high correlation in the way and degree in which OTC and NYSE stocks move. By the end of 1987 the total value of all NASDAQ issues was over $210 billion. The risk level of investing in OTC stocks is quite high. This index has a standard deviation of almost 24, versus 18 for the S&P 500. Surprisingly, this is less than that of the AMEX, which has a standard deviation of close to 28.

Additional Information

NASDAQ Company Directory. NASD Information Department, 1735 K Street, NW, Washington, DC 20006. (202) 728-8000.

OVER-THE-COUNTER COMPOSITE

Year	Year-End Close	Annual Change	Cumulative Total
1972	133.73	17.18%	17%
1973	92.19	-31.06%	-19%
1974	59.82	-35.11%	-48%
1975	77.62	29.76%	-32%
1976	97.88	26.10%	-14%
1977	105.05	7.33%	-8%
1978	117.98	12.30%	3%
1979	151.14	28.10%	32%
1980	202.34	33.87%	77%
1981	195.84	-3.21%	71%
1982	232.41	18.67%	104%
1983	278.60	19.87%	145%
1984	247.39	-11.21%	118%
1985	324.93	31.36%	185%
1986	348.83	7.36%	205%
1987	330.47	-5.26%	190%
1988	381.38	15.41%	234%

Average compound annual return for the last 17 years = 7.4%.

Standard and Poor's 500 Index

The Standard and Poor's 500 Index measures changes in stock market conditions based on the average performance of 500 widely held common stocks. Commonly known as the *S&P 500*, this index is overseen and published by the Standard and Poor's Corporation. The index tracks 400 industrial stocks (also called the *S&P 400*), 20 transportation stocks, 40 financial company stocks and 40 public utilities.

The S&P 500 is a market-value-weighted index showing the change in the aggregate market value of 500 stocks relative to the base period 1941–1943. Close to 94 percent of this index is made up of NYSE-listed companies, with some AMEX and OTC stocks. The index represents about 80 percent of the market value of all issues traded on the NYSE.

The S&P 500 is broad enough to capture most of the value in the U.S. equity market. Indeed, many money managers have compensation schedules based on how they fare against this index. The major shortcoming of the S&P 500 is that it measures only capital appreciation returns, not total returns. The accompanying graph and table *include* the reinvestment of dividends. Historically, nearly two thirds of the market's total return has been due to common stock dividends.

Additional Information

Standard and Poor's Corporation. 25 Broadway, New York, NY 10004. (212) 208-8690.

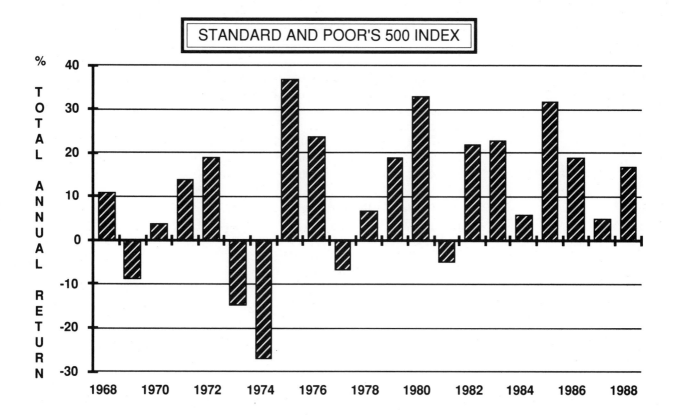

STANDARD AND POOR'S 500 INDEX

Year	Total Annual Return	Cumulative Total
1968	11%	11%
1969	-9%	1%
1970	4%	5%
1971	14%	20%
1972	19%	43%
1973	-15%	22%
1974	-27%	-11%
1975	37%	22%
1976	24%	51%
1977	-7%	40%
1978	7%	50%
1979	19%	79%
1980	33%	138%
1981	-5%	126%
1982	22%	176%
1983	23%	239%
1984	6%	259%
1985	32%	374%
1986	19%	464%
1987	5%	492%
1988	17%	593%

Average compound annual return for the last 21 years = 9.6% (includes reinvestment of dividends).

Standard and Poor's 500 Index Close

The following graph and table show the closing value of the S&P 500 over the past 20 years. These figures do not represent how one would have fared in the stock market. Closing index figures do not take into account the dividend yield of these stocks.

S&P 500 closing index numbers can be used to compare the performance figures of other indexes and averages that are reported without showing the impact of dividend payments.

Additional Information

Barron's. Subscriber Services, 200 Burnett Road, Chicopee, MA 01021-9988. (800) 345-8505.

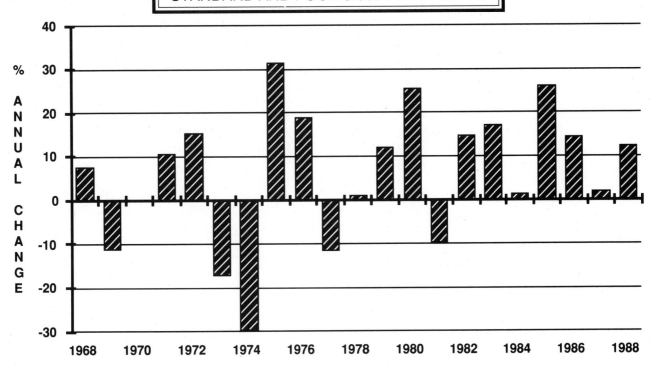

STANDARD AND POOR'S 500 INDEX CLOSE

Year	Year-End Close	Annual Change	Cumulative Total
1968	103.86	7.7%	8%
1969	92.06	-11.4%	-4%
1970	92.15	0.1%	-4%
1971	102.09	10.8%	7%
1972	118.05	15.6%	24%
1973	97.55	-17.4%	3%
1974	68.56	-29.7%	-28%
1975	90.19	31.5%	-5%
1976	107.46	19.2%	13%
1977	95.10	-11.5%	-1%
1978	96.11	1.1%	0%
1979	107.94	12.3%	12%
1980	135.76	25.8%	41%
1981	122.55	-9.7%	27%
1982	140.64	14.8%	46%
1983	164.93	17.3%	71%
1984	167.24	1.4%	73%
1985	211.28	26.3%	118%
1986	242.17	14.6%	151%
1987	247.08	2.0%	156%
1988	277.72	12.4%	187%

Average compound annual return for the last 21 years = 5.1% (without dividends reinvested).

Value Line Composite Index

The Value Line Composite Index is an equally weighted geometric average of approximately 1,700 NYSE, AMEX and OTC stocks. This index, which began in 1961, is monitored and adjusted by Value Line Investment Survey. The index is neither price- nor market-value-weighted.

Over the very long run, U.S. stocks have dramatically outperformed all types of bonds and other forms of debt instruments. One dollar invested in 1789 would have earned close to a nine percent annual compound return, and the money would have doubled roughly every eight years. Through the magic of compounding, investors would have made almost *five million* times their money in U.S. equities over the last 200 years.

Since the mid-1940s, returns on the riskiest equities, OTC stocks, have even surpassed those of the NYSE. The bull market of the early and late 1980s, however, showed the blue-chip stocks outperforming the over-the-counter issues.

Additional Information

Value Line. 711 Third Avenue, New York, NY 10017. (800) 633-2252.

VALUE LINE COMPOSITE INDEX

Year	Year-End Close	Annual Return	Cumulative Total
1968	183.2	19.8%	20%
1969	130.6	-28.7%	-15%
1970	103.6	-20.7%	-33%
1971	112.9	9.0%	-27%
1972	114.1	1.1%	-26%
1973	73.6	-35.5%	-53%
1974	49.0	-33.4%	-69%
1975	70.7	44.3%	-55%
1976	93.5	32.2%	-41%
1977	93.9	0.4%	-41%
1978	98.0	4.4%	-39%
1979	121.9	24.4%	-24%
1980	144.2	18.3%	-10%
1981	137.8	-4.4%	-14%
1982	158.9	15.3%	-1%
1983	194.4	22.3%	21%
1984	178.0	-8.4%	11%
1985	214.9	20.7%	34%
1986	225.6	5.0%	41%
1987	201.6	-10.6%	25%
1988	232.7	15.4%	44%

Average compound annual return for the last 21 years = 1.8% (does not include dividends).

Dow-Jones Industrial Average

The DJIA is a price-weighted average of 30 actively traded blue-chip stocks, primarily representing industrial companies. Prepared and published by Dow Jones and Company since 1884, it is the oldest and most widely quoted of all the market indicators.

The average's components, which change from time to time, represent close to 20 percent of the market value of all stocks listed on the NYSE. The DJIA is calculated by adding the closing prices of the component stocks and using a divisor that is adjusted for splits, dividends and issue substitution. The average is quoted in points, not in dollars.

The Dow tracks the market to a large extent and provides investors with an indication of short-term market trends. Unfortunately, the Dow measures only capital appreciation returns and does not include the reinvestment of dividends. Oftentimes, studies unfairly compare the stock market, using the DJIA, against other investment vehicles without including the additional returns provided by dividends. This is somewhat analogous to ranking the performance of income-producing real estate by just including the property's appreciation and ignoring the rent rolls.

Over the long term, the Dow has consistently underperformed the market as a whole because it covers only large companies and ignores dividend payments. During the last 60 years, dividends have represented nearly two thirds of the true *total* return from the stock market. The annual and compound returns shown below do not include the reinvestment of dividends.

The following 30 stocks comprise the DJIA:

Alcoa	McDonald's
Allied-Signal	Merck
American Express	Minnesota Mining
AT&T	Navistar
Bethlehem Steel	Philip Morris
Boeing	Primerica
Chevron	Procter & Gamble
Coca Cola	Sears Roebuck
Du Pont	Texaco
Kodak	Union Carbide
Exxon	United Technologies
General Electric	USX Corp.
General Motors	Westinghouse
Goodyear	Woolworth
IBM	
International Paper	

Additional Information

Dow Jones and Company. World Financial Center, 200 Liberty Street, Tower A, New York, NY 10281. (212) 416-2000.

DOW-JONES INDUSTRIAL AVERAGE

Year	Year-End Close	Annual Change	Cumulative Total
1968	943.75	4.3%	4%
1969	800.36	-15.2%	-12%
1970	838.92	4.8%	-8%
1971	890.20	6.1%	-2%
1972	1020.02	14.6%	13%
1973	850.86	-16.6%	-6%
1974	616.24	-27.6%	-32%
1975	852.41	38.3%	-6%
1976	1004.65	17.9%	11%
1977	831.17	-17.3%	-8%
1978	805.01	-3.1%	-11%
1979	838.74	4.2%	-7%
1980	963.99	14.9%	7%
1981	875.00	-9.2%	-3%
1982	1046.54	19.6%	16%
1983	1258.64	20.3%	39%
1984	1211.57	-3.7%	33%
1985	1546.67	27.7%	70%
1986	1895.95	22.6%	109%
1987	1938.83	2.3%	113%
1988	2168.57	11.8%	139%

Average compound annual return for the last 21 years = 4.2% (without dividends reinvested) and 9.7% (with dividends reinvested).

Dow-Jones Transportation Average

The DJTA is a price-weighted average of 20 railroad, airline and trucking stocks. The transports are calculated by adding the closing prices of the component stocks and using a divisor that is adjusted for splits, dividends and issue substitution. The average is quoted in points, not in dollars.

It has often been said that the stock market, as represented by the Dow-Jones Industrial Average, cannot sustain a significant upward trend without a corresponding move in the transportational stocks. The reasoning behind this statement is that the goods produced by the industrials must be physically moved by some form of transportation.

According to the *Dow theory*, a measurement device followed by some stock analysts who believe that future movement can be determined by past performance (a technical approach), a major trend in the stock market must be confirmed by a similar movement in the DJTA. The theory states that a significant trend is not confirmed until both Dow-Jones indexes (DJIA and DJTA) reach new highs or lows; if they do not, the market will fall back to its former trading range.

These 20 issues make up the DJTA:

Alaska Air Group	Norfolk Southern
AMR Corp.	North West Airlines
American President	Pan American
Burlington Northern	Ryder System
CSX Corp.	Santa Fe Southern Pacific
Carolina Freight	Southwest Air Lines
Consolidated Freightways	Union Pacific
Consolidated Rail	United Airlines
Delta Air Lines	US Air Group
Federal Express	XTRA Corp.

The annual and compound returns shown on the following table and graph do not include the reinvestment of dividends.

Additional Information

Dow Jones and Company. World Financial Center, 200 Liberty Street, Tower A, New York, NY 10281. (212) 416-2000.

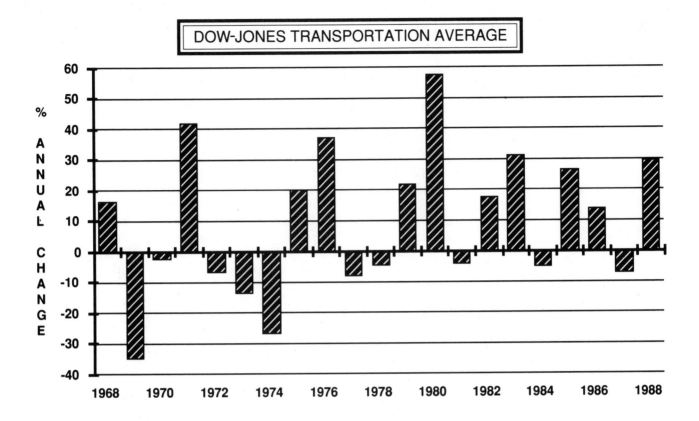

DOW-JONES TRANSPORTATION AVERAGE

Year	Year-End Close	Annual Change	Cumulative Total
1968	271.60	16.4%	16%
1969	176.34	-35.1%	-25%
1970	171.52	-2.7%	-27%
1971	243.72	42.1%	4%
1972	227.17	-6.8%	-3%
1973	196.19	-13.6%	-17%
1974	143.44	-26.9%	-39%
1975	172.65	20.4%	-27%
1976	237.03	37.3%	0%
1977	217.18	-8.4%	-8%
1978	206.56	-4.9%	-13%
1979	252.39	22.2%	6%
1980	398.10	57.7%	67%
1981	380.30	-4.5%	60%
1982	448.38	17.9%	89%
1983	589.59	31.5%	148%
1984	558.13	-5.3%	136%
1985	708.21	26.9%	200%
1986	807.17	14.0%	242%
1987	748.86	-7.2%	218%
1988	969.84	29.5%	313%

Average compound annual return for the last 21 years = 7.0% (without dividends reinvested).

Dow-Jones Utilities Average

The DJUA is a price-weighted average of 15 geographically representative gas and electric utility companies. The utilities average is calculated by adding the closing prices of the component stocks and using a divisor that is adjusted for splits, dividends and issue substitution. The average is quoted in points, not in dollars.

Utility stocks have historically been defined as high-dividend-paying securities that are relatively stable in price. These issues, excluding those companies that have nuclear power, are designed for the conservative investor.

Two of the biggest payments incurred by utility companies are energy costs and interest expenses. Besides purchasing or developing energy, utility companies have a very large debt structure to service, due to the amount of bonds and preferreds outstanding. The cost of servicing this debt is enormous. Thus, the level of interest rates is of a particular interest to utility companies. The Dow-Jones Utilities Average (DJUA) is oftentimes a barometer of what is occurring in the bond market. Normally, if the DJUA is moving up, so is the bond market; if utilities are off on any given day, bonds have usually also suffered a loss.

These 15 issues comprise the DJUA:

American Electric Power	Niagara Mohawk Power
Centerior Energy	Pacific Gas and Electric
Columbia Gas System	Panhandle Eastern
Commonwealth Edison	Peoples Energy
Consolidated Edison	Philadelphia Electric
Consolidated Natural Gas	Public Service Enterprises
Detroit Edison	SCE Corp.
Houston Industries	

The annual and compound returns shown on the following table and graph do not include the reinvestment of dividends. In this case, with such high-dividend-paying securities, this average dramatically downplays the true total return provided by utility issues.

Additional Information

Dow Jones and Company. World Financial Center, 200 Liberty Street, Tower A, New York, NY 10281. (212) 416-2000.

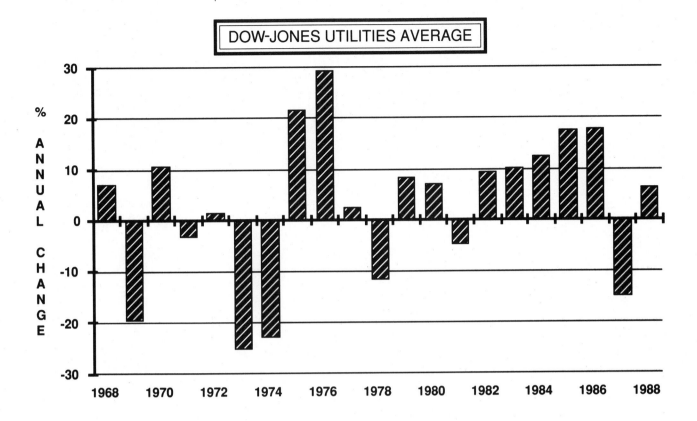

DOW-JONES UTILITIES AVERAGE

Year	Year-End Close	Annual Change	Cumulative Total
1968	137.17	7.2%	7%
1969	110.08	-19.7%	-14%
1970	121.84	10.7%	-5%
1971	117.75	-3.4%	-8%
1972	119.50	1.5%	-7%
1973	89.37	-25.2%	-30%
1974	68.76	-23.1%	-46%
1975	83.65	21.7%	-34%
1976	108.38	29.6%	-14%
1977	111.28	2.7%	-11%
1978	98.24	-11.7%	-22%
1979	106.60	8.5%	-15%
1980	114.42	7.3%	-9%
1981	109.02	-4.7%	-14%
1982	119.46	9.6%	-5%
1983	131.84	10.4%	5%
1984	148.52	12.7%	19%
1985	174.81	17.7%	40%
1986	206.01	17.9%	65%
1987	175.08	-15.0%	40%
1988	186.28	6.4%	48%

Average compound annual return for the last 21 years = 1.9% (without dividends reinvested).

EAFE Stock Index

The letters *EAFE* stand for Europe, Australia and the Far East. This weighted index is the most widely used measurement of the performance of stock markets outside the United States. The six countries that comprise the majority of this index are: Japan (62 percent), United Kingdom (16 percent), West Germany (eight percent), France (five percent), Italy (three percent) and the Netherlands (three percent).

A strong case can be made for investing overseas, both in terms of performance and risk. During each of the last five years, the EAFE has outperformed the S&P 500. In 17 of the past 25 years the EAFE has outpaced the U.S. stock market. Excluding dividends, the EAFE Index went up nearly four times as much as the S&P 500.

Over the past quarter century the U.S. stock market, excluding dividends, has had a negative return only six times: 1966 (-13 percent), 1969 (-13 percent), 1973 (-19 percent), 1974 (-31 percent), 1977 (-12 percent), and 1981 (-9 percent). In each of those six years an investor would have done better by investing in foreign markets. Over two thirds of the world's stocks are listed on foreign exchanges.

Foreign markets constitute a large share of world equity value. During the last several years, their share of the worldwide equity market has increased rapidly. In 1960 U.S. stocks represented 67 percent of the world's equity value. By 1988 the U.S. share dropped to 28 percent. The market pie has grown much bigger and foreign markets have increased their percentage of the whole.

In the past quarter century, the Pacific Basin has had a compound annual return of close to 17 percent, compared with about ten percent for the United States. Long-term predictions are difficult to make, but because of its human resources, technology and work ethic, the Pacific Basin looks like a very good bet over the next dozen years.

If you were to chart the top five performing stock markets around the world over the past ten years, making a chart of 50 separate slots, the U.S. stock market would only appear once. In 1982, the United States had the second-best-performing stock market. Of the 19 top-performing stock markets around the world, the Unites States is ranked 16th on an average annual compound basis since 1970.

Additional Information

First National Bank of Chicago, Business and Economic Research Division. One First
   National Plaza, Chicago, IL 60670. (312) 732-3779.

EAFE STOCK INDEX

Year	Annual Change	Cumulative Total
1974	-25.6%	-26%
1975	31.2%	-3%
1976	-0.4%	-3%
1977	14.6%	12%
1978	28.9%	44%
1979	1.8%	47%
1980	19.0%	75%
1981	-4.9%	66%
1982	-4.6%	58%
1983	20.9%	91%
1984	5.0%	101%
1985	53.0%	208%
1986	66.8%	414%
1987	24.9%	543%
1988	26.7%	717%

Average compound annual return for the last 15 years = 15.0% (without dividends reinvested).

Australian Stock Market

Close to 1,200 stocks are traded on the six Australian exchanges. The two largest securities markets are located in Melbourne and Sydney. Due to the wealth of the country's natural resources, almost one third of the equities traded represent mining companies.

There are two trading sessions during the week, 10:00 A.M. to 12:15 P.M. and 3:00 P.M. to 5:00 P.M. Brokerage fees are now negotiable. Last year the daily trading volume averaged over 70 million shares. The value of all Australian stocks, in U.S.-dollar terms, is approximately $100 billion.

Interest received by nonresidents is subject to a ten percent withholding tax; dividends earned by foreigners are taxed at 15 percent.

During the last decade the Australian stock market has had three outstanding years. In 1979 and 1980 it was the fourth-best-performing market in the world, up 42 percent and 52 percent respectively, Australia ranked number three in 1983, up 53 percent. All of these returns, as well as those on the accompanying table and graph, are in U.S.-dollar terms. The U.S. dollar is used for consistency; one foreign investment cannot be properly measured against another investment unless a single currency is used for comparison purposes.

Additional Information

Morgan Stanley Capital International Perspective. Morgan Stanley, 1633 Broadway, New York, NY 10019.

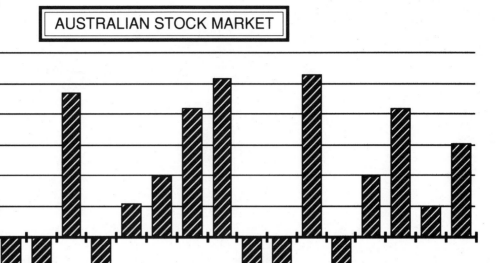

Year	Annual Return	Cumulative Total
1970	-19%	-19%
1971	-8%	-25%
1972	20%	-10%
1973	-12%	-21%
1974	-32%	-46%
1975	47%	-21%
1976	-10%	-29%
1977	11%	-21%
1978	20%	-5%
1979	42%	35%
1980	52%	105%
1981	-23%	58%
1982	-22%	23%
1983	53%	88%
1984	-13%	64%
1985	20%	97%
1986	42%	180%
1987	10%	208%
1988	30%	300%

Average compound annual return for the last 19 years = 7.6%.

Canadian Stock Market

There are five stock exchanges in Canada. The Toronto (TSE) and Vancouver stock exchanges represent the two largest security marketplaces. The Canadian stock markets are more familiar to U.S. investors than any other foreign market. The Toronto exchange serves as a major trading place for mining and energy penny stocks. This exchange has recently increased its activity in industrial issues.

The Canadian equity market has a large number of natural resource and mining company stocks. Trading volume averages close to ten million shares a day, valued at approximately $65 million in U.S.-dollar terms. The major indexes used to measure performance in the Canadian equity market are the General Index, which contains 85 issues, and the TSE 300 Composite Index, which contains 300 stocks.

Brokerage fees are negotiable on the Canadian exchanges. Dividends received by foreign citizens are subject to a 15 percent withholding tax; interest is taxed at a flat ten percent rate. U.S. citizens receive a tax credit for any Canadian interest and dividend taxes withheld.

During the last ten years, Canada has been ranked in the top-performing world markets twice. In 1979 it was the third-best-performing market with a return of 50 percent. In 1987 it was the fourth-best-performing market with a return of 14 percent. All of these gains, as well as those returns shown in the accompanying table and graph, are in U.S.-dollar terms.

Additional Information

Federal Reserve Bank of New York, Public Information Department. 33 Liberty Street, New York, NY 10045. (212) 791-6134.

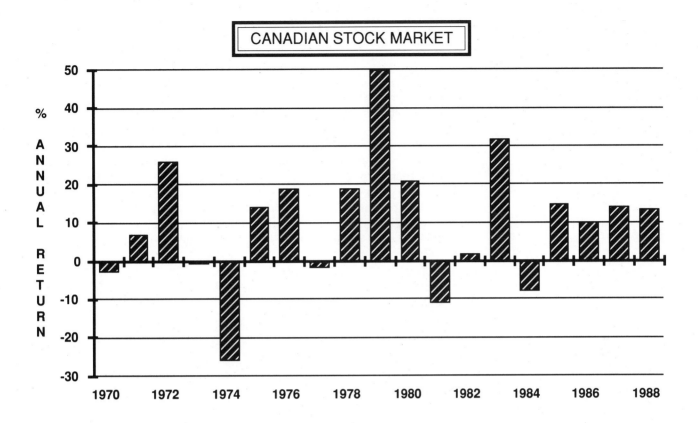

Year	Annual Return	Cumulative Total
1970	-3%	-3%
1971	7%	4%
1972	26%	31%
1973	-1%	30%
1974	-26%	-4%
1975	14%	9%
1976	19%	30%
1977	-2%	27%
1978	19%	51%
1979	50%	127%
1980	21%	175%
1981	-11%	145%
1982	2%	150%
1983	32%	230%
1984	-8%	204%
1985	15%	250%
1986	10%	285%
1987	14%	339%
1988	13%	396%

Average compound annual return for the last 19 years = 8.8%.

French Stock Market

There are seven stock exchanges in France. Average daily trading volume is over $25 million. Total market capitalization is approximately $700 billion in U.S.-dollar terms. The French equity market is the third largest in Europe. The largest exchange is the Paris Bourse, which originated in the 1500s. The major index used to measure performance in the French equity market is the Compagnie des Agents de Change (CAC) Index, which includes 262 issues.

Interest earned by foreign citizens is taxed at ten to 12 percent. Dividends are subject to a 15 percent income tax. In the past, France has had some rather innovative securities, including bonds denominated in railway tickets and securities valued by the price of gold bullion.

In 1978 France was the top-performing market in the world with a gain of 68 percent. During 1979 it had the fifth-best market with a return of 27 percent. During 1985 and 1986 France ranked fifth each year, with returns of 86 percent and 81 percent, respectively. All of these returns, as well as those shown on the next table and graph, are in U.S.-dollar terms.

Additional Information

Federal Reserve Bank of New York, Public Information Department. 33 Liberty Street, New York, NY 10045. (212) 791-6134.

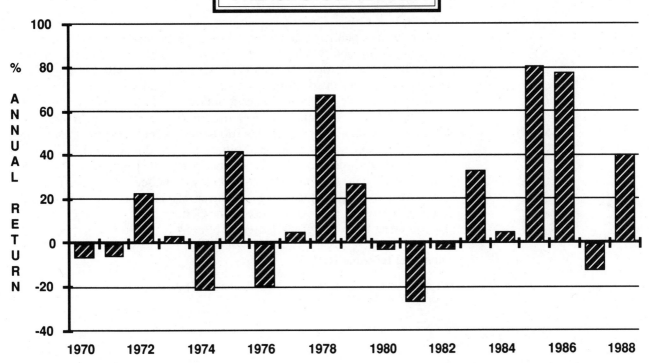

Year	Annual Return	Cumulative Total
1970	-7%	-7%
1971	-6%	-13%
1972	23%	7%
1973	3%	10%
1974	-22%	-14%
1975	42%	22%
1976	-20%	-2%
1977	5%	3%
1978	68%	73%
1979	27%	120%
1980	-3%	113%
1981	-27%	55%
1982	-3%	50%
1983	33%	100%
1984	5%	110%
1985	81%	280%
1986	78%	576%
1987	-13%	488%
1988	40%	723%

Average compound annual return for the last 19 years = 11.7%.

West German Stock Market

West Germany's publicly traded stock market is small compared with its huge debt and *private* equity market. Yet Germany's public stock market is the second largest in Europe. The market is decentralized, with the Frankfurt exchange dominant in fixed-income and international securities. The Düsseldorf exchange is strong in domestic industrial stocks. The major index used to measure performance in the German equity market is the Frankfurter Allgemeine Zeitung, which includes 100 issues. In mid-1988 the total value of German stocks was close to $210 billion in U.S.-dollar terms.

From 1978 through 1987 West Germany has been one of the top-performing world markets only once. In 1985 it was the second-best performer, with a gain of 133 percent in U.S.-dollar terms. There is only a moderate correlation between the performance of the German and U.S. stock markets. The following table and graph represent returns in U.S.-dollar terms.

Additional Information

Federal Reserve Bank of New York, Public Information Department. 33 Liberty Street, New York, NY 10045. (212) 791-6134.

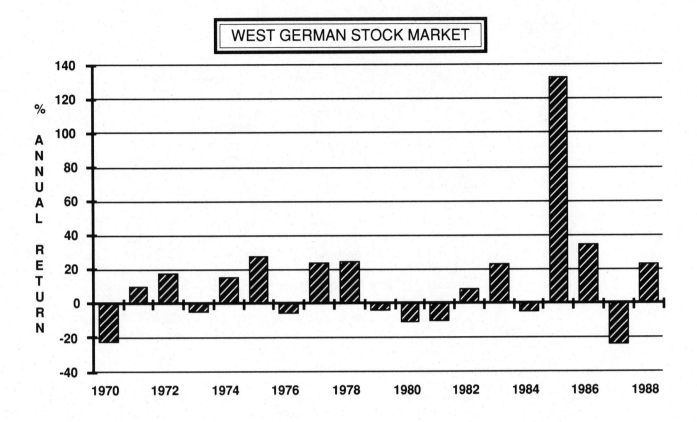

WEST GERMAN STOCK MARKET

Year	Annual Return	Cumulative Total
1970	-23%	-23%
1971	10%	-15%
1972	18%	0%
1973	-5%	-5%
1974	16%	10%
1975	28%	41%
1976	-6%	33%
1977	24%	65%
1978	25%	106%
1979	-4%	98%
1980	-11%	76%
1981	-10%	58%
1982	9%	72%
1983	23%	112%
1984	-5%	101%
1985	133%	368%
1986	35%	532%
1987	-24%	380%
1988	23%	490%

Average compound annual return for the last 19 years = 9.8%.

Hong Kong Stock Market

Hong Kong has a highly volatile stock market, subject to extreme price swings. Stock prices crashed in 1973–1974, but quickly turned around and averaged a 40 percent annual compound rate of growth for the balance of the 1970s. After the 1975–1979 rally the market plunged in 1981 and 1982, when diplomatic talks stalled between the United Kingdom and China over the colony's future. When an agreement was reached in the mid-1980's, stating that the colony will become part of China in 1997, with the right to maintain a marketplace based on capitalism for at least 50 years, the Hong Kong stock market took off once again.

Singapore's is perhaps the only stock market that is more volatile than Hong Kong's. At close to 57, Hong Kong's standard deviation is greater than that of gold bullion or metals funds. The correlation between the exchanges in Hong Kong and the United States is on the high side, at .6 (a perfect correlation is 1.00). The correlation between Hong Kong and Japan is similar.

There are four exchanges in Hong Kong. The combined value of the equities on these four exchanges was over $65 billion in U.S.-dollar terms in mid-1988. The major index used to measure performance in the Hong Kong equity market is the Hang Seng Index.

During the last ten years the Hong Kong stock exchange has been one of the two top-performing markets in the world three times. In 1979 it was up 80 percent and it was up 71 percent in 1980. Four years later, in 1984, Hong Kong had the best-performing stock market in the world, up 45 percent. All of these gains are in U.S.-dollar terms.

Additional Information

Far East Economic Review. Centre Point, 181 Glouchester Road, Hong Kong.

HONG KONG STOCK MARKET

Year	Annual Return	Cumulative Total
1970	42%	42%
1971	76%	150%
1972	151%	528%
1973	-38%	289%
1974	-54%	79%
1975	106%	269%
1976	40%	417%
1977	-11%	360%
1978	18%	443%
1979	80%	877%
1980	71%	1571%
1981	-16%	1304%
1982	-42%	714%
1983	-2%	698%
1984	45%	1057%
1985	50%	1636%
1986	54%	2573%
1987	-4%	2466%
1988	23%	3056%

Average compound annual return for the last 19 years = 19.7%.

Italian Stock Market

The Italian stock market, situated in Milan, saw an almost-uninterrupted drop from the early 1960s to 1977. The 1980s have seen an impressive growth rate in Italian stocks, but they remain at the bottom of the pack in long-run performance. Since 1970 Italy has ranked 15th in world equity markets, just slightly above the performance of the U.S. market. Only during the past several years has Milan been considered a major stock market.

Over 150 equities are listed on the exchange in Milan. The major index used to measure performance in the Italian equity market is the Milan Banca Italiana (MIB) historical index, which contains 129 issues. Total stock market capitalization at the end of 1987 was $84 billion. The standard deviation (risk) of the Italian stock market is twice that of the United States.

Over the last ten years Italy has had some remarkably good years, ranking as one of the top-performing markets in the world four times. In 1978 it was ranked third (44 percent); first in 1980 (78 percent); third in 1985 (130 percent); and third in 1986 (107 percent). Over the past 25 years Italy has averaged an annual compound rate of approximately seven percent. All of these gains are in U.S.-dollar terms.

Additional Information

Review of Economic Conditions in Italy. Banco di Roma, Viale U. Tupini 180, 00144 Rome, Italy.

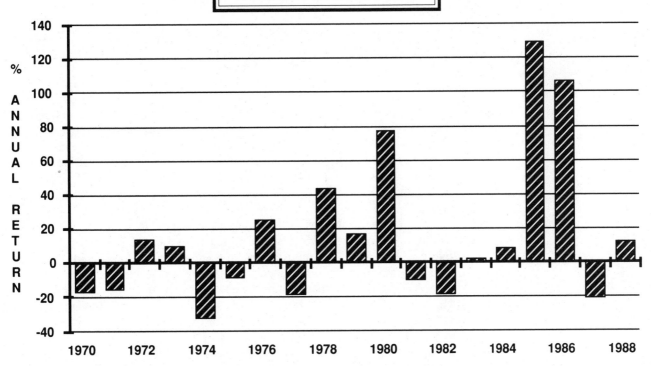

ITALIAN STOCK MARKET

Year	Annual Return	Cumulative Total
1970	-17%	-17%
1971	-16%	-30%
1972	14%	-20%
1973	10%	-12%
1974	-33%	-41%
1975	-9%	-46%
1976	26%	-32%
1977	-19%	-45%
1978	44%	-21%
1979	17%	-8%
1980	78%	64%
1981	-10%	48%
1982	-19%	20%
1983	3%	24%
1984	9%	35%
1985	130%	211%
1986	107%	544%
1987	-21%	409%
1988	13%	475%

Average compound annual return for the last 19 years = 9.6%.

Japanese Stock Market

There are eight stock exchanges in Japan. Tokyo and Osaka are the largest markets in trading volume. The major index used to measure equity performance on the Osaka exchange is the 300 Common Stock Index. The major indexes for the Tokyo exchange are the Tokyo Stock Price Index and the Nikkei Dow Jones.

The Tokyo Stock Exchange is larger than the NYSE in trading volume, and ranks with New York and London as one of the world's most widely followed markets. Approximately 1,600 companies are listed on the Tokyo Stock Exchange. Daily trading volume has averaged about 420 million shares in recent years, and total market capitalization is approximately $5.5 trillion as of mid-1988. The price of an average share of stock is approximately five dollars.

From 1960 to the mid-1980s, one dollar invested in Japanese equities would have grown to over $50, assuming reinvestment of dividends. This figure would be $134 if the time frame were expanded to the end of 1987. This performance far outdistances that of any other country in the world. United States and European equities were practically tied, with a dollar growing to about $11 in these two marketplaces from 1960 to 1985. It is interesting to note that the Japanese have had this amazing success in a relatively short period; in 1946 Japan's per capita income was $29 per year.

All stocks listed on the Japanese exchanges are subject to daily price limits that constrain the amount of a security's movement. There are two daily trading sessions on the Tokyo and Osaka stock exchanges, from 9:00 A.M. to 11:00 A.M. and from 1:00 P.M. to 3:00 P.M. A morning session is held on three Saturdays each month. Many Japanese stocks are traded in the United States, usually in the form of ADRs (American depository receipts).

Japanese tradition encourages companies doing business with one another to hold shares of each other's stocks. Thus, corporate holdings of other domestic stocks form an appreciable portion of Japan's aggregate equity value. Such holdings also increase the stability of the security's price.

In Japan transaction costs are fixed, although the commission schedule is changed from time to time. Nonresident foreign investors must appoint a resident of Japan to act as a proxy on his or her behalf. Interest and dividend income earned by nonresidents is subject to a 20 percent flat withholding tax. Thanks to tax treaties between Japan and the United States, this rate is reduced to ten percent to 15 percent for Americans.

Japan had the best overall market during the past ten years and the past 25 years. From 1978 through 1987, it ranked in the top four, five times. In 1978 it was ranked second (52 percent); fourth in 1981 (15 percent); third in 1984 (17 percent); fourth in 1986 (99 percent); and first in 1987 (43 percent). All of these figures are in U.S.-dollar terms.

Additional Information

Tokyo Stock Exchange Monthly. Tokyo, Japan.

Japan Economic Journal. Tokyo International, P.O. Box 5004, Tokyo, Japan.

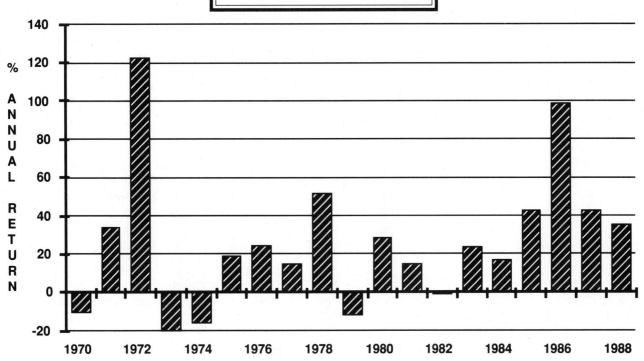

Year	Annual Return	Cumulative Total
1970	-11%	-11%
1971	34%	19%
1972	123%	165%
1973	-20%	112%
1974	-16%	78%
1975	19%	112%
1976	25%	165%
1977	15%	205%
1978	52%	364%
1979	-12%	308%
1980	29%	426%
1981	15%	505%
1982	-1%	499%
1983	24%	643%
1984	17%	769%
1985	43%	1143%
1986	99%	2374%
1987	43%	3438%
1988	35%	4676%

Average compound annual return for the last 19 years = 22.6%.

Mexican Stock Market

The stock market in Mexico was founded in 1894, but remained decentralized for several decades. In the 1970s the Mexican government established a central stock exchange in Mexico City, the Bolsa de Valores de Mexico. Trading on the Mexican market has been active only since 1976.

U.S. investors can buy and sell Mexican securities through U.S. brokers, or they may participate in mutual funds specializing in Mexican investments. In late 1987 the total stock market capitalization of Mexico was just slightly over $1 billion in U.S.-dollar terms.

During the past several years, Mexico's stock market has scored well during two periods. In 1983 the market was ranked first in the world, gaining 164 percent for the year, doubling the second-best-performing marketplace, Norway (82 percent). For 1986 Mexico was ranked second, with a return of close to 106 percent. These returns, as well as those shown on the accompanying table and graph, are in U.S.-dollar terms.

Additional Information

Federal Reserve Bank of New York, Public Information Department. 33 Liberty Street, New York, NY 10045. (212) 791-6134.

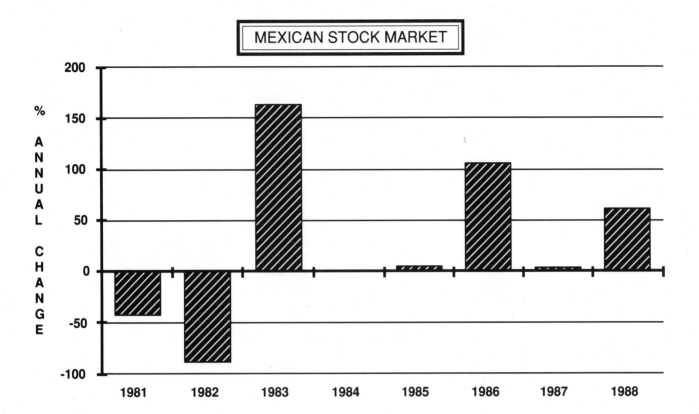

Year	Annual Change	Cumulative Total
1981	-42.9%	-43%
1982	-88.7%	-94%
1983	164.3%	-84%
1984	2.0%	-84%
1985	6.0%	-83%
1986	106.1%	-65%
1987	3.9%	-64%
1988	62.3%	-42%

Average compound annual return for the last 8 years = -6.6%.

Spanish Stock Market

Despite the ironclad rule of Francisco Franco, Spain emerged in the 1960s and early 1970s with a healthy economy, including a rapidly rising stock market. A signal given by a series of reforms in the late 1950s and early 1960s caused a large injection of foreign capital. Increased funds helped to stabilize and increase performance in the Spanish equity markets. Since the mid-1970s, returns have been quite mixed.

The two major exchanges in Spain are located in Barcelona and Madrid. The Barcelona exchange contains more than 425 issues and is measured by the General Index of Barcelona Stock Exchange (73 issues). The Madrid exchange contains more than 450 issues and is represented by the Madrid Stock Exchange Index (69 issues).

Twice during the past ten years, Spain has had one of the two top-performing equity markets in the world. In 1984 Spain was the second-best-performing market (36 percent) and in 1986 it had the number-one market in the world (117 percent).

Additional Information

Federal Reserve Bank of New York, Public Information Department. 33 Liberty Street, New York, NY 10045. (212) 791-6134.

SPANISH STOCK MARKET

Year	Annual Return	Cumulative Total
1970	-4%	-4%
1971	18%	13%
1972	40%	58%
1973	24%	96%
1974	-9%	78%
1975	0%	78%
1976	-35%	16%
1977	-33%	-22%
1978	6%	-17%
1979	4%	-14%
1980	3%	-11%
1981	11%	-1%
1982	-27%	-28%
1983	-6%	-32%
1984	36%	-8%
1985	51%	39%
1986	117%	202%
1987	36%	311%
1988	14%	369%

Average compound annual return for the last 19 years = 8.5%.

Swiss Stock Market

Switzerland has seven stock exchanges, of which the Zurich, Basel and Geneva exchanges account for the bulk of the country's securities trading. These three exchanges function essentially as one, since trades are executed wherever terms are most favorable. The Basel exchange is the eighth largest in the world. The Swiss stock market ranks fourth in size in Europe.

A high percentage of the Swiss equity market are bank shares and foreign companies. The shares of approximately 315 companies are listed on the seven exchanges. Only about one third of the stocks have markets large enough for institutional trading. Trading volume was about $300 billion U.S. dollars for the entire year of 1987. Total market capitalization was $136 billion dollars as of December 31, 1987. The major index used to measure stock performance in Switzerland is the Societe de Banque Suisse, which contains 90 issues.

Commissions in Switzerland are fixed according to a set schedule. Interest and dividends earned by foreign citizens is subject to a withholding tax that ranges from zero percent to 35 percent.

Only once during the past ten years has Switzerland had one of the best-performing stock markets. That was in 1985 when it had the number-four spot, with a return of 105 percent. Since 1970 it has ranked as the seventh-best-performing stock market in the world.

Additional Information

Federal Reserve Bank of New York, Public Information Department. 33 Liberty Street, New York, NY 10045. (212) 791-6134.

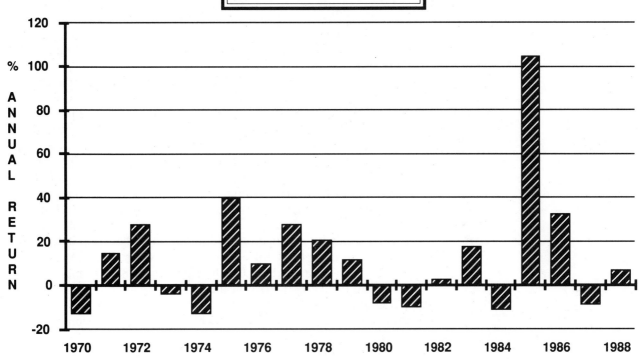

Year	Annual Return	Cumulative Total
1970	-13%	-13%
1971	15%	0%
1972	28%	28%
1973	-4%	23%
1974	-13%	7%
1975	40%	50%
1976	10%	65%
1977	28%	111%
1978	21%	155%
1979	12%	186%
1980	-8%	163%
1981	-10%	137%
1982	3%	144%
1983	18%	188%
1984	-11%	156%
1985	105%	425%
1986	33%	598%
1987	-9%	535%
1988	7%	579%

**Average compound annual return for the last
19 years = 10.6%.**

United Kingdom Stock Market

Of the 13 stock exchanges in the United Kingdom, only the London Stock Exchange (LSE) is of importance to foreign investors. The others are small and provincial in nature.

The London exchange is the central securities marketplace for the United Kingdom and the Republic of Ireland. It was formed in 1973 by consolidating all the regional stock exchanges with the old London Stock Exchange. The LSE was one of the oldest exchanges in the world, dating back to the 1600s.

The LSE lists approximately 2,800 companies, and by that measure is the world's largest. The list is large because almost any reputable security in any developed country can be listed. In fact, the list includes more than 100 NYSE and AMEX stocks. Moreover, fixed-income issues outnumber equities on the LSE. Although the British market is the largest in Europe, in equity value it is only about one seventh as large as the U.S. market.

The London Stock Exchange is the third largest in the world in terms of trading volume, trailing only Tokyo and New York. Total market capitalization was over one trillion U.S. dollars by the end of 1987. The major index used to measure the equity market in the United Kingdom is the Financial Times All Ordinaries Index.

Transaction costs are negotiated. Interest and dividend income earned by nonresidents is not subject to withholding tax.

The United Kingdom has been one of the top-performing markets in the world twice in the last decade. In 1980 Britain's stock market was ranked fifth (39 percent). In 1987 it was ranked third with a return of 35 percent.

Additional Information

Federal Reserve Bank of New York, Public Information Department. 33 Liberty Street, New York, NY 10045. (212) 791-6134.

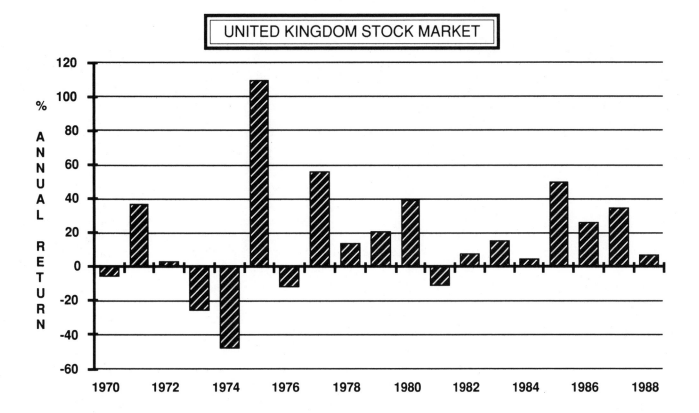

UNITED KINGDOM STOCK MARKET

Year	Annual Return	Cumulative Total
1970	-6%	-6%
1971	37%	29%
1972	3%	33%
1973	-26%	-2%
1974	-48%	-49%
1975	110%	7%
1976	-12%	-6%
1977	56%	47%
1978	14%	68%
1979	21%	103%
1980	39%	182%
1981	-11%	151%
1982	8%	171%
1983	16%	214%
1984	5%	230%
1985	50%	395%
1986	26%	524%
1987	35%	742%
1988	7%	801%

Average compound annual return for the last 19 years = 12.3%.

TANGIBLES

Rare United States Coins

Tangibles, which include rare coins, are one of the trickiest investments for investors. Due to the expertise required and the lack of regulation, tangibles are not recommended for most investors. An estimated 14 to 20 million Americans collect and invest in coins. However, the true marketplace for investment-grade coins involves a small fraction of this population.

The supply of investment-grade rare coins is quite small. The United States has the most highly regulated and popular coin market in the world. When purchasing coins for investment purposes, it is important that only coins graded by a truly independent and recognized source, such as the American Numismatic Association or Professional Coin Grading Service, are considered.

Rare coins are normally marked up, or have a bid-ask spread, that is several times greater than that found in the securities marketplace. The spread between the buy and sell price normally ranges from ten percent to 20 percent. For this reason, investors should plan on holding their coins for a minimum of five years.

The figures shown on the next table and graph represent how several categories of rare coins have performed as an average. The figures are provided by the *Coin Dealer Newsletter*, a publication widely used by coin dealers and collectors, and by *Coin World Trends*.

Additional Information

American Numismatic Association. P.O. Box 2366, Colorado Springs, CO 80901. (303) 632-2646.

The Coin Dealer Newsletter. P.O. Box 11099, Torrance, CA 90510. (213) 370-5579.

RARE UNITED STATES COINS

Year	Annual Change	Cumulative Total
1968	15.3%	15%
1969	1.4%	16%
1970	0.6%	17%
1971	9.9%	29%
1972	40.5%	82%
1973	56.1%	184%
1974	41.0%	300%
1975	10.4%	340%
1976	18.8%	424%
1977	18.6%	524%
1978	66.1%	935%
1979	202.4%	3125%
1980	80.4%	5627%
1981	-7.1%	5232%
1982	-15.2%	4447%
1983	31.9%	5902%
1984	11.2%	5562%
1985	50.6%	9960%
1986	11.5%	11167%
1987	-16.9%	9252%
1988	26.2%	1226%

Average compound annual return for the last 21 years = 13.1%.

Diamonds

The exact date of the discovery of diamonds is not certain. Manuscripts from India, dated 500 A.D., refer to diamond valuation. Some historians believe that these gemstones were first used by the Greeks and the Romans several hundred years before Christ.

Uses for diamonds have varied over time. Warriors, believing diamonds to be a means of protection, have worn the stones into battle. Diamonds have also been used in attempts to cure mental illness and the effects of poison.

The largest diamond-producing country is South Africa, although nearly all African nations have diamond deposits. Other countries that mine diamonds include Indonesia, the Soviet Union, Brazil, India and the United States.

Industry uses 75 percent of all diamonds produced. These gemstones conduct heat better than any known substance. Henry Ford was the first to discover that a diamond is the cheapest industrial abrasive for long-term use. Detroit has more diamond tool dealers than any other city in the world.

The gem market accounts for the remaining 25 percent of diamond sales. Stones weighing less than 0.2 carats are considered industrial. The "four Cs"—carat, color, cut and clarity—are used in grading and pricing diamonds. Yellow and brownish stones are considered undesirable; pink, blue, violet, green and white diamonds are sought after.

The Gemological Institute of America rates the color of diamonds. The term "perfect diamond" is used to describe a stone that reveals no flaws to the trained eye under a ten-power magnification.

Low-grade sizes of diamonds are crushed and made into powder that is used to coat drills, saws and other industrial materials. Gem diamonds are cut with a full 58 facets, small, polished surfaces that are square, rectangular or oval in shape.

Diamonds have been a very volatile investment, particularly over the past decade. In the early 1980s, high-quality gemstones dropped in value as much as 80 percent. On the other hand, industrial low-grade diamonds have had an impressive long-term record. In the early 1940s, industrial diamonds sold for as much as $1.75 per carat. Today, these same stones average $600 per carat. Long-term performance figures for gem diamonds have not proved to be reliable. In 1978, Michael Rapaport founded the *Rapaport Diamond Report* to set forth standards and to verify and record prices fairly and accurately. This weekly price list covers per carat prices of 1,280 categories of diamonds. Published in New York City, this eight-page report is unpopular in the industry because it prints reports of diamond price weaknesses when it occurs.

Investing in diamonds is quite tricky. Diamonds sold through jewelers and other retail sources are often marked up 100 percent or more. Recent discoveries of additional stones have clouded the future investment outlook. A 1985 discovery at the Argyle mines in Australia increased the world's supply by 60 percent. For the overwhelming majority of investors, diamonds should be purchased for their beauty alone, and not as a money-making vehicle.

Additional Information

The Official Investor's Guide: Buying and Selling Gold, Silver and Diamonds. House of Collectibles, Inc. 1900 Premier Row, Orlando, FL 32809. (407) 857-9095.

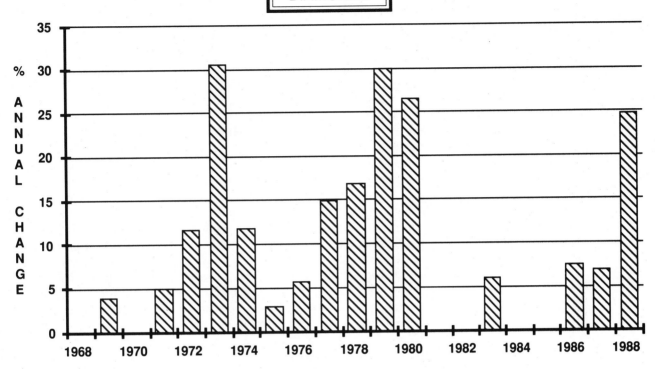

DIAMONDS

Year	Annual Change	Cumulative Total
1968	0.0%	0%
1969	4.0%	4%
1970	0.0%	4%
1971	5.0%	9%
1972	11.7%	22%
1973	30.6%	60%
1974	11.9%	79%
1975	3.0%	84%
1976	5.7%	95%
1977	15.0%	124%
1978	17.0%	162%
1979	30.0%	241%
1980	26.6%	333%
1981	0.0%	333%
1982	0.0%	333%
1983	6.1%	359%
1984	0.0%	359%
1985	0.0%	359%
1986	7.5%	396%
1987	7.0%	431%
1988	24.8%	564%

Average compound annual return for the last 21 years = 9.4%.

Gold

Gold has shown itself as an amazing store of value over the last several centuries. With an ounce of gold a man or woman has always been able to buy a fine suit of clothing.

During the Civil War the United States used paper money. Due to the inflationary effects of war, gold prices doubled to $42 per ounce. By 1878 the price of the bullion had gone back to its prewar level of $20. The Gold Standard Act of 1900 gave gold official recognition in relation to the dollar. The act stayed intact until 1971. In the early 1930s Congress made owning gold illegal. From 1934 to 1971 the dollar was vaguely measured in gold, the value being set by the U.S. Treasury.

Since the abolition of the Gold Standard Act in 1971, the price of gold has been extremely volatile. From a price of $35 per ounce in early 1968, gold jumped to more than $800 per ounce for a very brief period in 1980.

Despite sporadic spikes in price, gold's *long-term* purchasing power has remained steady. Because gold's purchasing power is normally steady, gold investments historically have had a real return near zero. Silver prices have paralleled gold prices and also have had an inflation-adjusted return near zero. Although these metals do not have positive real returns in the long run, gold is useful as an *insurance asset* to diversify against catastrophic events and to hedge against inflation.

In Great Britain the annual compound *real* return (growth minus inflation) from gold over the last four centuries has been one tenth of one percent per year. In the United States it has been seven tenths of one percent over the past two centuries. This means that gold prices and commodity indexes track one another over the long run. In short, gold has been a good representative of general commodity indexes.

The quantity of gold, relative to other metals, is low, while the demand for it is comparatively high. Consequently, gold's total value is about 1/22 of the world's wealth. A high percentage of the world's gold is tied up in the reserves of central banks, but more than half is outside governmental control.

Gold's standard deviation, or variance of return, is close to 30. Such a high standard deviation is noteworthy; it makes gold the second or third most volatile investment. On a more positive note, the correlation between gold and stocks, or bonds, is negative. A negative correlation coefficient means that investments normally move in opposite directions. Thus, gold is an excellent way to diversify an investment portfolio.

Additional Information

Gold Information Center. 900 Third Avenue, New York, NY 10022. (212) 688-0474.

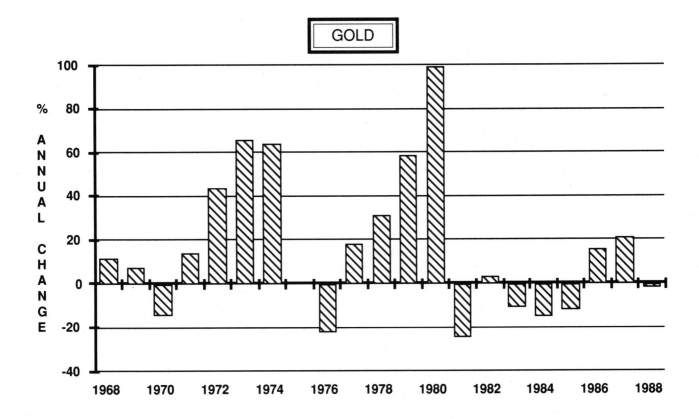

Year	$/Ounce	Annual Change	Cumulative Total
1968	$39	11.4%	11%
1969	$42	7.7%	20%
1970	$36	-14.3%	3%
1971	$41	13.9%	17%
1972	$59	43.9%	68%
1973	$98	66.1%	179%
1974	$161	64.3%	358%
1975	$161	0.0%	358%
1976	$125	-22.4%	257%
1977	$148	18.4%	321%
1978	$194	31.1%	452%
1979	$308	58.8%	778%
1980	$613	99.0%	1647%
1981	$460	-25.0%	1210%
1982	$476	3.5%	1249%
1983	$424	-10.9%	1101%
1984	$360	-15.1%	921%
1985	$317	-11.9%	798%
1986	$368	16.1%	942%
1987	$447	21.5%	1161%
1988	$437	-2.2%	1136%

Average compound annual return for the last 21 years = 12.7% (dollar-per-ounce figures represent yearly averages).

United States Crude Oil Prices

The United States consumes more oil and gas than any other nation—nearly one third more than Italy, Spain, France, West Germany, Great Britain, Japan and Canada combined. Approximately 30 years ago, the United States produced enough oil and gas to meet domestic needs and lead the world in exports. Today the United States imports several million barrels a day from foreign sources.

Most direct investments in oil programs are designed for investors who: (1) need tax deductions, (2) have no immediate need for income from the investment, (3) have adequate liquid assets and current income to bear the risk of loss and (4) are emotionally able to wait a long time before realizing returns.

A barrel represents 42 gallons of oil. One barrel of crude oil has the Btu (British thermal unit) equivalence of 6,000 cubic feet of natural gas. The Btu is a measure of the energy value of petroleum products.

Additional Information

Chase Manhattan Bank, Energy Economics Department. 1 Chase Manhattan Plaza, New York, NY 10015. (212) 552-2222.

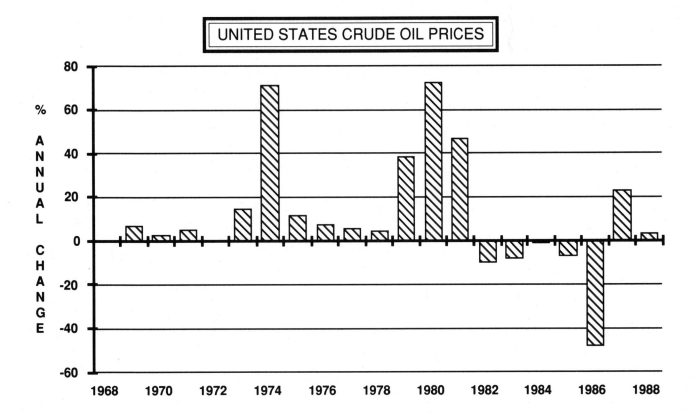

UNITED STATES CRUDE OIL PRICES

Year	Average Price per Barrel	Annual Change	Cumulative Total
1968	$2.9	0.7%	1%
1969	$3.1	6.9%	8%
1970	$3.2	3.2%	11%
1971	$3.4	5.4%	17%
1972	$3.4	0.0%	17%
1973	$3.9	14.7%	35%
1974	$6.7	71.8%	132%
1975	$7.5	11.9%	160%
1976	$8.1	8.0%	181%
1977	$8.6	6.2%	198%
1978	$9.0	4.7%	213%
1979	$12.5	38.9%	335%
1980	$21.6	72.8%	653%
1981	$31.8	47.2%	1007%
1982	$28.5	-10.4%	896%
1983	$26.2	-8.1%	816%
1984	$25.9	-1.1%	807%
1985	$24.1	-6.9%	744%
1986	$12.5	-48.1%	339%
1987	$15.4	23.2%	440%
1988	$16.0	3.9%	462%

Average compound annual increase for the last 21 years = 8.6%.

Old Masters

In the last several years, art prices appear to have followed those of other investment vehicles in the marketplace. When the stock and bond markets are strong, the art market generally follows suit. The art world is particularly closely associated with the Japanese stock market, since the Japanese are now the biggest buyers of art. In 1987, two Van Gogh paintings sold for $39.9 and $53.9 million, respectively — the highest prices ever paid for auctioned art. One painting was acquired by a Japanese company, the second by an Australian investor.

Sotheby's, an international art dealership located in London and founded in 1744, sells more than 500,000 pieces of art annually at its fine arts auctions. Total value of these works exceeds $1 billion.

Dealers who purchase art at auction generally mark up the price 100 percent when they retail the work in their galleries.

The typical art investor has $50,000 to spend. Good paintings from the eighteenth century can still be bought for $2,500 to $10,000. Experts state that old masters *drawings* appreciated 2,100 percent between 1951 and 1969, and that old masters paintings went up 38-fold during the same time frame. Commissions for selling art can range anywhere from 10 percent to 40 percent or more.

The Old Masters Paintings Index is a listing of works painted before the nineteenth century. The most expensive items are excluded from the index because such scarce works are not representative of the market. Also, the least expensive material is left out because it is not of interest to serious collectors. The accuracy of this index, which is based on "results of auction sales by affiliated companies and other information deemed relevant by Sotheby's," is debatable. However, the index is constantly being refined.

Prospective investors should stay abreast of scandals, fakery and short-lived cycles in the art world. In 1981, the president of Christie's, another major dealer in old masters paintings, admitted that the reported sale of two French Impressionist paintings never occurred. Their quoted prices had been used to beef up the prices of similar works. A New York couple was convicted of selling over $1.3 million worth of fake Dalis. The day before Andy Warhol died, one of his pictures had an estimated value of less than $6,000. Soon after his death, it sold for $40,000. The buyer later resold the picture for $75,000.

Like most other collectibles, fine art should be purchased for aesthetic, not money-making, purposes. The pricing and valuation of old masters paintings is more tricky than that of diamonds, rare coins or stamps. Markups can be astronomical, not to mention the high cost of insurance premiums. There is an old saying in investing worth heeding: "Never invest in something that needs to be housed or fed."

Additional Information

National Antique and Art Dealers Association of America, Inc. 15 East 57th Street. New York, NY 10022. (212) 355-0636.

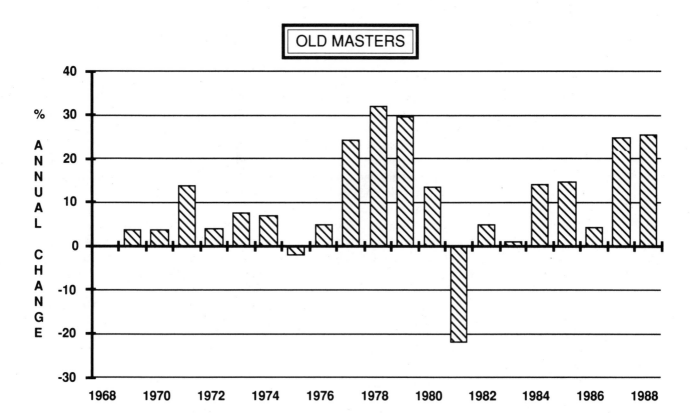

Year	Annual Change	Cumulative Total
1968	0.0%	0%
1969	4.0%	4%
1970	3.8%	8%
1971	13.9%	23%
1972	4.1%	28%
1973	7.8%	38%
1974	7.2%	48%
1975	-2.0%	45%
1976	5.2%	52%
1977	24.5%	90%
1978	32.1%	151%
1979	29.7%	226%
1980	13.8%	272%
1981	-22.0%	190%
1982	5.2%	205%
1983	1.3%	208%
1984	14.2%	251%
1985	14.9%	304%
1986	4.5%	324%
1987	23.1%	422%
1988	25.7%	558%

Average compound annual return for the last 21 years = 9.4%.

Platinum

Platinum, discovered 500 years ago, is the rarest precious metal on earth. To date, only 2,300 tons of the metal have been mined versus 100,000 tons of gold. Today, only 85 tons of platinum are mined annually versus 10,000 tons of silver and 1,000 tons of gold.

Approximately 90 percent of all platinum mined comes from South Africa, five percent from the Soviet Union and the remaining portion from the United States and Canada. Three South African mining companies, Rustenberg, Impala and Western, produce 80 percent of the Western world's supply of platinum.

Approximately 30 percent of all the platinum produced is used in jewelry. While the demand in industry, defense and technology rises, only four percent of annual platinum production is acquired by investors, versus 54 percent of gold's annual production. The small investor base makes this a very volatile investment.

Platinum is the only metal that has traded above $1,000 per ounce. Its all-time high was in 1980, when it briefly hit $1,047 per ounce. It can be purchased in one-ounce and ten-ounce bars, as well as in coin form as legal tender from the Isle of Man and New Zealand.

Additional Information

International Precious Metals Institute. Government Building, ABE Airport, Allentown, PA 18103. (215) 266-1570.

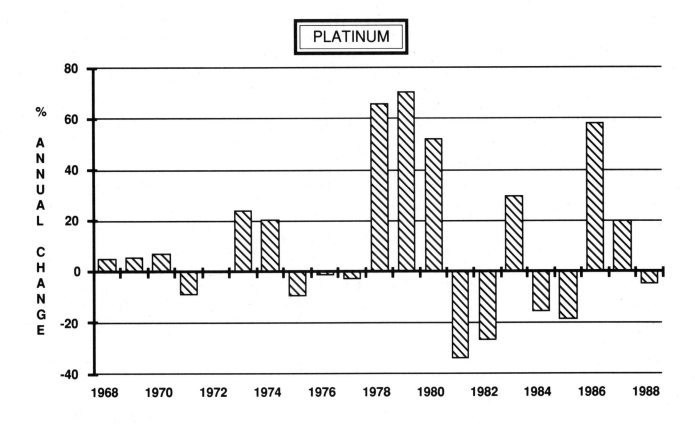

Year	$/Ounce	Annual Change	Cumulative Total
1968	$117	5.4%	5%
1969	$124	6.0%	11%
1970	$133	7.3%	19%
1971	$121	-9.0%	8%
1972	$121	0.0%	8%
1973	$150	24.0%	34%
1974	$181	20.7%	62%
1975	$164	-9.4%	47%
1976	$162	-1.2%	46%
1977	$157	-3.1%	42%
1978	$261	66.2%	136%
1979	$445	70.5%	304%
1980	$677	52.1%	514%
1981	$446	-34.1%	305%
1982	$327	-26.7%	196%
1983	$424	29.7%	285%
1984	$357	-15.8%	223%
1985	$291	-18.5%	165%
1986	$461	58.4%	319%
1987	$553	20.0%	403%
1988	$525	-5.1%	378%

Average compound annual return for the last 21 years = 7.7% (dollar-per-ounce figures represent yearly averages).

Real Estate Investment Trusts (REITs)

REITs manage a portfolio of real estate or mortgages to earn profits for shareholders. Certain REITs specialize in a geographical area. Others concentrate on structure type or use.

Equity REITs purchase real estate. Shareholders get rental income from the properties and receive capital gains as buildings are sold. Such equity participation does not provide the same level of current income found in mortgages, which generally do not have appreciation potential.

Mortgage REITs specialize in lending money to builders and developers. Interest income received is passed on to shareholders. Some REITs, referred to as *hybrid*, have a mix of equity and debt instruments. Equity REITs have greater upside potential than their mortgage counterparts.

REITs are usually publicly traded companies whose shares are traded on the NYSE, AMEX or OTC. Over 100 different REITs are currently traded. Some REITs do not have an active secondary market and are difficult to sell.

Investors are attracted to REITs because they offer a means of owning real estate or mortgages, while having the marketability of stocks. Equity REITs can be an excellent way to diversify one's portfolio.

Over the past 40 years, *unleveraged* residential real estate has had a compound annual return of close to eight percent; unleveraged business property has averaged close to 8.5 percent. The standard deviation, or volatility, of all cash real estate has been 3.71. The standard deviation for U.S. stocks has been four times as great. Since 1947 common stocks have outperformed unleveraged real estate by a ratio of almost 2.5 to one. Leveraged real estate has slightly outperformed common stocks.

During the last ten years the return on institutional real estate portfolios has equaled close to 15 percent on an annual basis. This is very close to the returns found in the S&P 500 over this same time frame, and almost 50 percent greater than bonds.

There is a very low correlation between real estate and the stock or bond market. There is a moderately high correlation between the performance of property and U.S. Treasury bills. And there is a very strong relationship between the rate of inflation and the growth rate of real estate.

Residential, business and farmland real estate represents slightly more than 50 percent of the entire wealth of the United States. In global terms, U.S. property represents 20 percent of the entire world's wealth. Real estate outside of the United States equals almost 40 percent of the more than $33 trillion global pie.

Additional Information

Bechtel Information Services. 15740 Shady Grove Road, Gaithersburg, MD 20877. (800) 231-DATA.

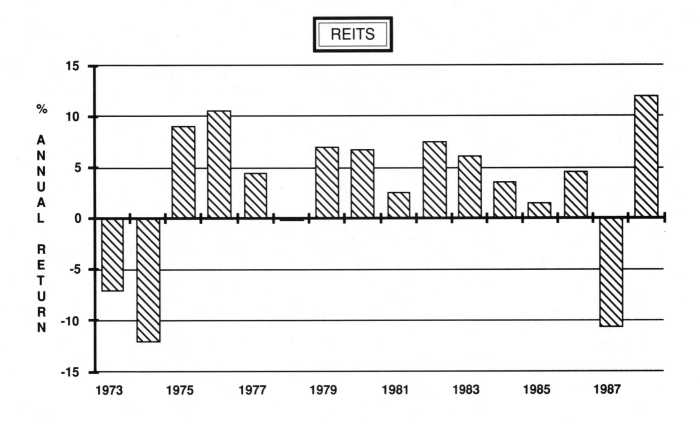

Year	Annual Return	Cumulative Total
1973	-7.1%	-7%
1974	-12.1%	-18%
1975	9.1%	-11%
1976	10.7%	-1%
1977	4.5%	3%
1978	-0.3%	3%
1979	7.1%	10%
1980	6.8%	18%
1981	2.6%	22%
1982	7.6%	32%
1983	6.2%	40%
1984	3.6%	46%
1985	1.6%	49%
1986	4.6%	56%
1987	-10.7%	39%
1988	12.0%	56%

Average compound annual return for the last 16 years = 2.8%.

Silver

The aggregate value of silver is only about 1/70 the aggregate value of gold. Consequently, the market for silver is very thin compared with the market for gold. Historically, silver and gold prices move together, with peaks and troughs at approximately the same time. In the past, approximately 35 ounces of silver have bought one ounce of gold. Recently an ounce of gold has been worth 65 ounces of silver.

Silver's highest year-end price was $28 per ounce in 1979. For a few days in January 1980, however, silver sold at above $50 per ounce. "Silver Thursday" is the day in 1980 when the Hunt brothers were unable to come up with $100 million to cover their silver futures contracts, causing the price of the metal to tumble.

The Western industrialized nations used roughly 420 million ounces of silver last year. This figure represents nearly 80 percent of total demand. Photography alone accounts for more than 40 percent of annual demand. Mexico is the largest producer; Peru is second in world silver output. Together, Mexico and Peru account for more than 30 percent of the world's silver production.

Mine output provides about 65 percent of the annual demand for silver. The rest comes from secondary sources such as recycled film, old jewelry and obsolete electronic gadgets.

One of the major arguments for including gold or silver in a portfolio comes from the diversification of risk it can provide. Low correlations with other assets make an asset a powerful diversification tool. For the last 25 years there has been a negative correlation between metals and U.S. stocks and bonds. Gold appears to be a better diversifier because it has much less price volatility and greater demand than silver.

Additional Information

The Silver Institute. 1001 Connecticut Avenue, Washington, DC 20036. (202) 331-1227.

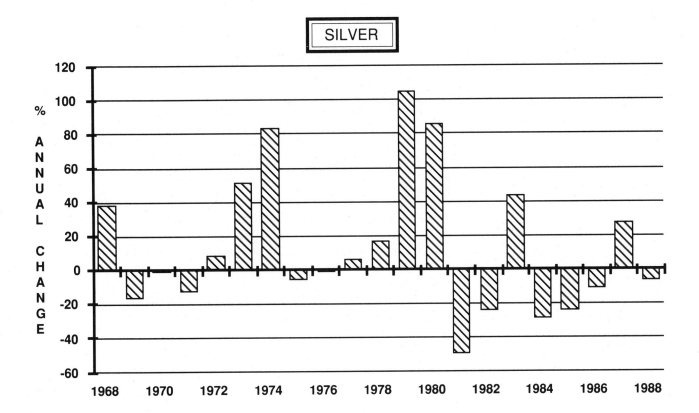

Year	$/Ounce	Annual Change	Cumulative Total
1968	$2.15	38.71	39%
1969	$1.79	-16.74	15%
1970	$1.77	-1.12	14%
1971	$1.55	-12.43	0%
1972	$1.69	9.03	9%
1973	$2.56	51.48	65%
1974	$4.71	83.98	204%
1975	$4.42	-6.16	186%
1976	$4.35	-1.58	180%
1977	$4.62	6.21	197%
1978	$5.40	16.88	247%
1979	$11.09	105.37	611%
1980	$20.63	86.02	1222%
1981	$10.48	-49.20	574%
1982	$7.95	-24.14	412%
1983	$11.44	43.90	637%
1984	$8.14	-28.85	423%
1985	$6.14	-24.57	292%
1986	$5.47	-10.91	249%
1987	$7.01	28.15	347%
1988	$6.54	-6.70	316%

Average compound annual return for the last 21 years = 7.0% (dollar-per-ounce figures represent yearly averages).

Rare United States Stamps

There are close to 30 million stamp collectors in the United States. Because stamp collecting is the largest hobby in this country, stamps, compared to other collectibles, are relatively marketable.

The first factor affecting a stamp's price is its scarcity; condition is the second major characteristic that should be examined. Coloration and "centering," as well as the amount and quality of perforation surrounding the design, are also important considerations. Obviously, uncancelled stamps, those that have original gum, and those never hinged are more valuable than their counterparts.

An advantage of investing in rare stamps and coins is their 1031 tax-free exchange. Named after Internal Revenue Code Section 1031, Reg. 1.1031(a)-1, a qualified 1031 exchange means that no gain or loss is recognized upon sale if the property being exchanged is like in kind and is held either for business or investment. Furthermore, on a somewhat different note, investors and collectors do not need to use their social security numbers when buying or selling rare coins and stamps.

Additional Information

U.S. Tangible Investment Corporation. 311 Market Street, Dallas, TX 75202.
   (214) 742-2200.
American Philatelic Society. P.O Box 8000, State College, PA.

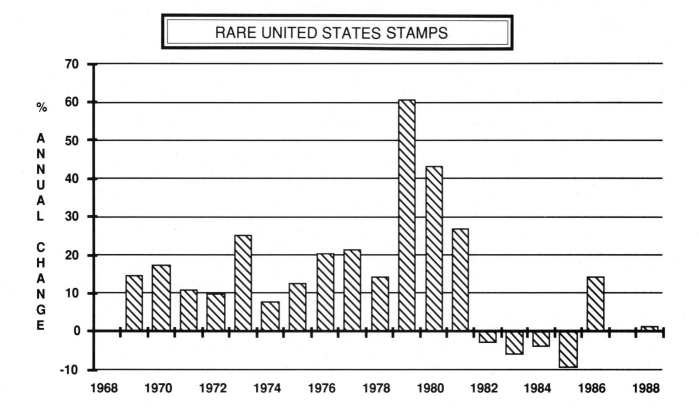

RARE UNITED STATES STAMPS

Year	Annual Change	Cumulative Total
1968	0.0%	0%
1969	14.6%	15%
1970	17.4%	35%
1971	11.0%	50%
1972	9.9%	65%
1973	25.4%	106%
1974	8.0%	122%
1975	12.6%	151%
1976	20.5%	204%
1977	21.4%	268%
1978	14.5%	323%
1979	60.9%	581%
1980	43.2%	874%
1981	27.0%	1,137%
1982	-3.0%	1,100%
1983	-6.0%	1,028%
1984	-4.0%	983%
1985	-9.6%	875%
1986	14.5%	1,021%
1987	0.5%	1,032%
1988	1.4%	1,043%

Average compound annual return for the last 21 years = 12.3%.

About The Author

Gordon K. Williamson, JD, MBA, CFP, CLU, ChFC, RP, is one of the most highly trained investment counselors in the United States. Dr. Williamson, a former tax attorney, is a Certified Financial Planner and branch manager of a national brokerage firm. He has been admitted to the Registry of Financial Planning Practitioners, the highest honor one can attain as a financial planner. He holds the two highest designations in the life insurance industry, Chartered Life Underwriter and Chartered Financial Consultant. He is also a real estate broker, with an MBA in real estate syndication.

Dr. Williamson is the author of several books, including *Investment Strategies, Survey of Financial Planning* and *Tax Shelters*. He has been the financial editor of various magazines and newspapers and a stock market consultant for a California television station.

Dr. Williamson has taught investment and financial planning classes at the University of California and California State University. He lives in La Jolla, California, and is president of an investment advisory firm.

INDEX